NORTH
KOREA

NORTH KOREA

UNMASKING
THREE GENERATIONS
OF MAD MEN

LIGHTNING
GUIDES

ISBN Print 978-1-942411-64-2
eBook 978-1-942411-65-9

> **"Only when peace is ensured can the people
> create an independent new life."**
>
> **—KIM IL-SUNG, 1991**

When Kim Jong-un decided to have his uncle Jang Song-thaek executed for alleged conspiracy, the leader of North Korea opted to feed his relative to a pack of attack dogs, or at least that was the story that immediately caught the world's attention. The international media, already accustomed to the outlandish claims of the Kims' propaganda machine, latched onto this nugget of information as another example of Kim Jong-un's maniacal mindset. Like nearly every milestone in the lives of the members of the Kim family—the dictatorial dynasty that has ruled North Korea since its inception—there are multiple versions of this story. It's true that Jang Song-thaek was executed, but the dogs were a sensational stretch. A Chinese tabloid first reported the supposed grisly method of death, an idea that started as a cartoon on a satirical Chinese blog.

The Korean peninsula's history is one of extreme subjugation, both political and cultural. Beginning in the 17th century, a then-united nation under the Choson Dynasty was nominally independent but subordinate to China. In 1910 Japan annexed the country, an occupation that only ended with Japan's surrender to the Allies in 1945. Korea became the gameboard in a war where

North and South were surrogates for the Soviet Union and the United States, respectively. The Korean war ended with an armistice that divided the peninsula in two.

Led by Kim Il-sung, Kim Jong-il, his son, and now Kim Jong-un, his grandson, the nation has suffocated within a cult of personality where North Korea is their heavily armed playground and Korean heritage begins and ends with their history. While South Korea has become a democracy and a powerful world economy, Il-sung and his successors have put North Korea in a straitjacket of state-owned industry that relies on forced prison labor. With a regime of terror that makes disloyalty the most severe crime and fills the gulags, North Koreans themselves are effectively imprisoned in their own country. The potent mix of totalitarian control and misinformation that hallmark the Kims' rule makes it possible to believe that a high-ranking government official would be turned into dog food. Understanding North Korea, and the three generations of men who have created it, is an exercise in parsing reality from carefully crafted myth.

CONTENTS

first, a few facts

In North Korea, people are allotted food, homes, and education according to their class: loyal, wavering, or hostile

North Korea's annual GDP per capita was US $1,800 in 2013

NORTH KOREA WITHDREW FROM THE TREATY FOR THE NON-PROLIFERATION OF NUCLEAR WEAPONS

North Korea tied with Somalia for the most corrupt country in the world, according to Transparency International's 2014 Corruption Index

People accused of political crimes may be imprisoned or executed without formal charges or trial

How was the Korean peninsula split into two countries?

At the end of World War II, Korea was under Japanese control. When Japan surrendered to the Allies, the United States and the Soviet Union were ideologically divided over what kind of government to establish in Korea. Their disagreements were contributing factors to the Korean War, which lasted until 1953. The armistice to end the conflict resulted in a demilitarized zone at latitude 38°N and the formation of sovereign nations on either side.

What is the "cult of personality"?

The cult of personality refers to the cultural hegemony of the Kim Dynasty, which has ruled North Korea dictatorially since its founding. The Kim Dynasty strictly prohibits all forms of personal expression, and has created a mythology to elevate Kim Il-sung and Kim Jong-il to demigod status.

Are there political parties in North Korea?

There are officially three political parties in North Korea: the Workers Party, the Chondoist Chongu Party, and the Korean Social Democratic Party. The Workers Party, however, exercises total authority over all of the other political parties.

How do elections work?

During election season, ballots list the Workers Party candidate as the single choice. Anyone wishing to elect a different candidate must say so publicly, but such an action would assuredly lead to imprisonment or worse.

What are the two main tenets of North Korean society?
Juche and *songun*. Juche is a policy of self-containment and self-reliance that cuts North Korea off from outside trade and business. Songun, the principle that values military power and the rule of the elite over all aspects of society, reinforces juche by mandating that all resources be funneled to the army.

Is there religious freedom in North Korea?
Technically yes, but in practice no. The constitution grants citizens freedom of religion, but few risk the consequences "of exercising that putative choice. Fortune-telling, however, enjoys wide popularity, as there is a strong belief in spirits.

How does the economy function?
North Korea is a self-contained socialist economy. In theory, this means that goods and services are produced within the country and distributed evenly to all citizens. However, the economy is under chronic stress, and most goods are produced by forced labor.

Is there cell phone or Internet service?
Only to a very limited extent. Some of the elite in Pyongyang have cell phones, but they can only make local calls. The country has an internal network for the Internet, and monitors individuals' search histories very carefully.

Can I travel there?
The US Department of State strongly advises Americans *against* traveling to North Korea. However, Americans can visit the country with a North Korean travel visa if they book a North Korean–run tour in advance. Once they land in North Korea, however, tour guides will carefully monitor where they go and what they see.

THE JAPANESE TAKEOVER

JAPAN'S 35-YEAR OCCUPATION DOMINATED ALL ASPECTS OF KOREAN LIFE

K orea became a colony of Japan on August 29, 1910, bringing an official end to the 518-year-old Choson Dynasty. While the Choson Dynasty was occupied with internal affairs in the 19th century, Japan was rapidly industrializing and building a powerful military. Japan's victory in the Sino-Japanese War (1894–95) undermined Chinese efforts at expansion and conquest, and its subsequent victory over Russia in the Russo-Japanese War (1904–05) demonstrated immensely powerful naval capabilities. Consequently, the world suddenly viewed Japan as a cultural portal into the rest of Asia. The Japan-Korea Annexation Treaty of 1910 brought Korea under the paternalistic wing of Japan, providing the land and resources Japan needed to expand its defensive perimeter onto mainland Asia.

Japan's colonizing mission surpassed mere territorial occupation. The occupiers sought to reform what they viewed as antiquated and evil Korean customs, and to effectively assimilate Koreans into Japanese society. The imperial elite viewed Korea as a kind of lost child of the Japanese empire. Using its new world prominence, imperial propagandists attempted to indoctrinate the world about Korean "backwardness," and Japanese hosts pointed out Korean racial and cultural "weaknesses" to Western visitors in Korea.

Despite Japanese efforts to quell any budding nationalism in Korea, the occupiers could not erase the memory of the many indignities they had forced on the Korean people. Material improvements in infrastructure and banking did not compensate for the violation of civil liberties, harsh taxes on tobacco and wine, government-mandated cash crop cultivation, and strict censorship laws.

Left: The landing of the *Unyo* in Korea, 1877

Japanese imperialism had imposed regulations on every aspect of Korean life, including how to bury the dead, slaughter livestock, gather firewood, and practice traditional medicine. Korean nationals did not easily bow to subjugation, however, and March 1919 brought forth a series of massive demonstrations known collectively as the March First Movement.

On March 1, 1919, leaders of the resistance gathered in Seoul to read the recently drafted Declaration of Independence. Korean crowds shouted "*Daehan minguk manse!*" meaning "Long live Korea!" The recitation had just begun, however, when Japanese authorities apprehended the leaders. Korean demonstrators were arrested, tortured, killed, or sent into exile. Beyond the imperial borders, rogue Korean groups with Soviet armaments coalesced to form the *Dongnipgun*, or Korean Independence Movement. The Dongnipgun trained in southern Manchuria with tacit approval from China and was headed by Yi Dong-hwi, a former commander of the long-suppressed *uibyong* resistance army. Although the Dongnipgun was far better developed than the small uibyong armies of the late Korean Empire, the Japanese maintained their dominance.

International Korean movements for independence included the formation of the Korean Provisional Government in Shanghai in April 1919. As its first order of business, the government sent an envoy to the Paris Peace Conference to galvanize Western support for Korean independence. At the conference, copies of the Korean Declaration of Independence were circulated to the delegates. Unfortunately, America, Britain, France, and Italy had no interest in making an enemy of Japan by supporting the disenfranchised Korean people. The delegates' response knocked Korean

Right: Gojong, the first Emperor of Korea (left); portrait of Emperor Meiji from the Imperial Printing Bureau

independence off the international agenda, and Korea's cause would not make headlines again until the end of World War II.

Although the March First Movement did not achieve independence for Korea, the Japanese government did make some concessions to improve the Korean people's quality of life. Prime Minister Hara Takashi, who had taken power in 1918, held a pragmatic approach to colonial policy. Takashi dismissed Hasegawa Yoshimichi, a severe and unyielding military ruler, and he appointed the more compassionate Admiral Saito Makoto. Saito implemented a cultural policy that would lighten Korean cultural restrictions, provide Koreans with better education and employment opportunities, and grant limited freedom of expression. Additionally, the policy guaranteed that demonstrations similar to the March First Movement would never occur again. To this end, the cultural policy made public order its first priority and enhanced police forces throughout the peninsula.

Korean agriculture benefited from the new reforms, and in 1920 Japan launched a massive campaign to increase rice production in Korea. Irrigation and drainage works were improved, crop rotation principles were employed, and an agricultural administration supervised the application of new seed strains. All the while, an increasingly high Japanese demand for rice stimulated market growth. With new money swelling through Korea, roads were paved, ports were built, and the coastal villages of Incheon, Wonsan, Naju, Kunsan, and Mokpo grew.

The Japanese concessions suddenly stopped when the conservative Tanaka Giichi was appointed Prime Minister in 1927, amid a Japanese movement toward asserting further control in the region. The Japanese enforced harsh new restrictions in Korea: It became illegal to teach the Korean language, and Koreans were forced to adopt Japanese names. Beyond the borders, Tanaka saw a budding threat in the Korean rebels residing in Manchuria with their Chinese compatriots, and, in 1931, he invaded Manchuria, consolidated it as part of the Japanese Empire, and installed a ruthless regional government aimed at subjugating Japan's "enemies."

KIM IL-SUNG EMERGES

One such enemy of the state was a 19-year-old by the name of Kim Song-ju. With his staunchly Korean-nationalist parents, Song-ju fled from the Pyongyang region to Manchuria in 1920. In 1926

Beginning in 1392, the Choson Dynasty ruled the peninsula now known as Korea. Favoring Confucianism over Buddhist principles, the Choson Dynasty achieved heights of culture, science, and trade in its early centuries. After Manchurian armies invaded in the mid-seventeenth century, however, Choson became a tributary state of neighboring China and its Qing Dynasty. The dynasty met its end when Japan annexed Korea in 1910.

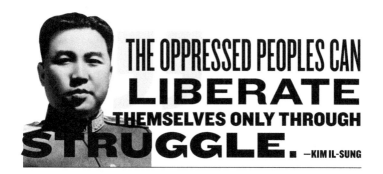

THE OPPRESSED PEOPLES CAN
LIBERATE
THEMSELVES ONLY THROUGH
STRUGGLE. ▪ —KIM IL-SUNG

he formed the Down with Imperialism Union to fight Japanese imperialism and promote the communist ideals of the Soviet Union.

Communist sentiment ran high in Manchuria in the late 1920s and early 1930s. In 1931 Song-ju, by then a member of the Communist Party of China, grew increasingly concerned about an imminent and inevitable Japanese invasion. He believed, rightly, that anything could provoke the Japanese. On the night of September 18, 1931, a small explosive detonated in close proximity to a Japanese railroad in Manchuria; it caused no casualties or serious equipment damage. Looking for an excuse to enter Manchuria, however, Japan called it an offensive strike and surged across the border.

Song-ju, angered by the invasion and stirred to an even greater sense of nationalism because of it, decided to adopt the nom de guerre Kim Il-sung. In one of his first actions as Il-sung, he joined the Northeast Anti-Japanese United Front, where he rose to the rank of major.

Kim Il-sung's war victories were modest but meaningful to Korean independence. In 1937 he was commander of a guerilla unit that successfully subdued Japanese imperialists crossing the Amnok (Yalu) River into China. For a few hours, Il-sung was even able to occupy a Japanese-held town immediately across the border. This small success was momentous for Koreans. Il-sung's brief conquest boosted Korean and Chinese morale, and he was rewarded with a promotion to United Army Commander. Il-sung's new position made him a pressing target for Japan in the early 1940s, and the Soviet Union assisted in hiding him in Siberia, where he served in the Soviet Red Army as a major until Japan surrendered to the Allies in World War II.

The period of Japanese occupation was a hugely conflicted time for the Korean people, one of significant economic progress and complete social oppression. The lasting effects of this dichotomous history are still felt: many Koreans hold that the country would have achieved the same advancements without Japan's interference. Perhaps the most significant event in the long run was the emergence of Kim Il-sung, who would soon completely reshape the future of his country.

THE ROOTS OF DIVISION

AFTER JAPAN SURRENDERS, THE ALLIES IMPOSE A PLAN

Today's North-South Korean border at the 38th parallel was originally drawn at a late-night meeting in Washington, DC, on August 10, 1945—years before the end of the Korean War. American and Soviet delegates, sensing that Japan's surrender was inevitable, had convened to discuss the issue of Korea. Despite their conflicting policies and ideologies, the United States and the Soviet Union had a stake in placating each other. With the war's end, territories that once fell under German or Japanese control would open up throughout Europe and Asia. Playing fair, at this juncture, was the name of the game. In the August 10 meeting, the superpowers decided on a joint occupation, allocating 37,055 square miles to the United States below the hastily drawn 38° 0´ N border and 48,191 square miles to the Soviet Union above it.

Neither the United States nor the Soviet Union were fully satisfied with the agreement. The Soviets wanted control of the entire peninsula, and the Americans were circumspect about beginning any occupation at all. The Allies, however, had already decided to provide assistance to Korea at the 1943 Cairo Conference, and although they were skeptical about how this assistance would carry through, they were clear about this: their ultimate goal was to give Korea back to the Koreans.

Despite their lengthy discussions at Cairo and Washington, the Soviet Union and the United States engaged in continuing power struggles over Korea between 1945 and 1948.

THE SOVIETS BRING KIM IL-SUNG HOME

By the summer of 1945, the Korean people had also sensed that Japan was ready to surrender. In preparation for their long-awaited liberation, Korean towns and cities formed local committees, which came under the purview of the Committee for the Preparation of Korean Independence (CPKI). The CPKI and the various local committees both held the shared goals of land reform, modernization, and social mobility.

A small, 21-man subsection of the Committee, led by Cho Man-sik, met the Soviet forces that entered Pyongyang on August 24, 1945. The Soviets fortified the group by adding their own

Korean cadres, and the CPKI became the local mouthpiece for Soviet interests in North Korea. The committee also assigned communists as top-tier administrators in education, military, propaganda, and government. These leaders made up the early communist Korean Workers' Party, and Kim Il-sung, who had returned to North Korea on September 19, was appointed as the party leader.

The Soviets trusted Kim Il-sung immediately. As party leader, Il-sung dominated North Korean politics. The Soviets boosted his growing political power with a massive propaganda campaign to build a "cult of personality" around Il-sung, a widely praised guerilla war hero who had risked his life for Korea. In addition, opponents were silenced by gunfire or exile, while only Il-sung and his officers were allowed to carry arms. This effectively positioned North Korea on the path toward totalitarianism.

Progress in the South did not move as swiftly. The United States accepted the surrender of Japanese troops in Seoul on September 9, 1945, one week after Japan's formal surrender. From the beginning, Americans had been reluctant to go into Korea and, unlike the Soviets, they did not have a connection to the land or the people. There were no South Korean cadres comparable to the Soviet-sponsored Korean cadres of the North, nor did they have a well-known figure like Il-sung to support. As the Americans looked for a leader, the most important criteria for the United States Army Military Government in Korea was that the leader speak English, have a dominant personality, and be Western-educated.

January 4, 1946 Cho Man-sik publicly expressed his upset over the trusteeship in a meeting of North Korea's People's Committee, was placed under house arrest, and soon disappeared.

Wall mural of Kim Il-sung, titled "Victorious Fatherland," Liberation War Museum, Pyongyang

A FUTILE MOVE TOWARD UNITY

In December 1945, the United States, the Soviet Union, and Great Britain met in Moscow to discuss Korea. The three nations agreed to establish a five-year trusteeship over a unified Korea, but this decision satisfied neither the United States nor the Soviet Union. Despite their opposition and respective concerns, however, both sides expressed public support for the trusteeship. North Koreans did so under pressure from Moscow, and the Americans did so because they had no alternative solution for the Korean nationalists who wanted immediate independence.

Efforts to unite Korea under one government were ephemeral. A Joint American-Soviet Commission met on one occasion in January 1946, and the discussion ended in a stalemate. This pleased the Soviet Union, which had made significant progress in establishing a communist regime above the 38th parallel. Starting in February 1946, the North Koreans chartered a well-organized path to one-party statehood under the North Korean Workers' Party. A Provisional People's Committee convened to discuss the economic and political foundation of a North Korean government, and Kim Il-sung was deeply involved in this process; he purged all opposition until his was the only name on the election ballot. In 1948, the nascent Supreme People's Assembly promulgated a legally binding constitution, and proclaimed the establishment of the Democratic People's Republic of Korea on September 9. With its newly afforded nation status, the People's Republic was left to govern itself. The Soviet Union withdrew.

As the northern government coalesced to form the foundation of modern-day North Korea, civil unrest in the South over famine and workers' strikes was derailing American efforts to organize. The US Army Military Government handled these issues by ramping up the police force across the country, in a move that echoed the Japanese occupation. Rebellions against the police broke out, and the US Military Government blamed the dissent on communist sentiment. Communist factions certainly existed in the South, but their tactics were more calculated and politically oriented than skirmishes with the police. The US occupiers tortured and killed protesters in the name of eliminating communism from South Korea.

With little hope of uniting the disparate political factions of the South, the United States approached the United Nations for help. US leaders were anxious to leave Korea as soon as possible (specifically, before March 31, 1948, a date on which the United

States had proposed that elections be held) but could not do so until the final transfer of power was made to a fully functioning Korean government. To expedite the process, the United Nations formed the UN Temporary Committee on Korea. The Temporary Committee helped South Korea elect its first president. The most popular name on the ballot, Syngman Rhee, was staunchly anti-communist: He spoke English, was well-traveled, and valued the American ideals of capitalism and democracy. In large part due to his American-backed campaign, Rhee was democratically elected in a landslide victory as the first president of the Republic of Korea. At last, the United States could begin to disengage from Korea.

Though both North and South were hoping for a unified Korea, the ideological tensions between the pro- and anti-communists were ultimately too powerful. In the short time between the establishment of the Democratic People's Republic in the north and the Republic of Korea in the south, it became increasingly clear that each side would try to overtake the other. The conflict—one as much between the Soviet Union and the United States as between North and South Korea—cost millions of lives and cemented in place a division that brought chaos to one side and prosperity to the other.

PAIN BY PROXY

WAS THE KOREAN WAR REALLY ONE BETWEEN THE UNITED STATES AND SOVIET UNION?

Before sunrise on Sunday, June 25, 1950, the Soviet-backed Korean People's Army (KPA) launched a strike on Ongjin Peninsula, across the border in South Korea. Their enemies—South Korean soldiers and American troops stationed in Ongjin—were on weekend leave. The KPA speedily moved on to Seoul and took the southern capital, without resistance, in only a few hours. The UN Security Council was swift in its condemnation of North Korea's invasion. Within a matter of days, the KPA's army had captured almost all of the neighboring South, formally known as the Republic of Korea.

North and South Korea had been antagonistic of each other since their incorporation in 1948, agreeing only on their desire for Korean unification. Unification, however, carried a different meaning for each side. Stalinism, the mainstay of the North, did not

Left: Painting of American soliders being defeated by North Korean and Chinese armies in the Korean War displayed at Friendship Tower, Pyongyang

General Douglas MacArthur arrived in the plane *Bataan* at the Kimpo airport in Seoul, August 14, 1948, from Tokyo, to attend the inauguration of the Republic of Korea.

fit South Korean president Syngman Rhee's democratic vision for Korea. Likewise, the Americanized Rhee did not reflect the values of Kim Il-sung and the North. Surprisingly, the KPA offensive was supported by the Soviet Union, which had been wary of antagonizing the United States after World War II. In fact, Il-sung and southern communist Pak Hon-yong had traveled to Moscow in 1949 to persuade Stalin that military action was needed. After seven months of correspondence Stalin had agreed to back the KPA, on the condition that Chinese leader Mao Zedong agree to go in, too. China might not have been allies with the Soviet Union, but it could be counted on to defend its shared border with North Korea; in the unchecked tension of the Cold War, defending a common border and political ideology took precedence over holding a grudge.

In the South, a hastily organized United Nations Command, headed by US General Douglas MacArthur, backed the army. The UN Command was a hasty solution to the well-developed KPA, which by 1950 had grown to an army of 800,000 men with Soviet weaponry and a firm conviction in the "Great Leader" Kim Il-sung. Il-sung had recruited his men through the Korean Workers' Party, a wide-reaching social infrastructure of "Kimists" with influence in every town, school, factory, and government building north of the 38th parallel. By contrast, the South was a sociopolitical

April 11, 1951 General Douglas MacArthur, who had undermined the Truman administration on many occasions, was relieved of his Korean command by Truman himself.

COMMON GROUND

During the civil war between the Kuomintang, or Chinese Nationalist Party, and the communist-led People's Republic, Mao Zedong conscripted a large contingent of skilled North Korean militia into the Chinese People's Liberation Army. In turn, these men formed the vanguard of the Korean People's Army in its effort to unite Korea, as well, under a communist-led government.

miscellany of political parties whose disunity often escalated to acts of terror. At the civil level, Koreans in the South experienced deep economic instability, resulting in homelessness, crime, inflation, food shortages, and electricity outages. Rhee's weak leadership and worsening domestic conditions kept the South from building a military force comparable to the KPA.

In the summer of 1950, American and South Korean forces secured a small defensive perimeter around the southern city of Pusan, deterring the North's advancement. The UN Command and the South Korean army prepared to invade Inchon in September. General MacArthur held that it was necessary to extend the fighting all the way into China, a belief that eventually cost him his position. With the invasion of Icheon, the South gained momentum and steadily pushed north, beyond the 38th parallel, toward the Chinese border at the Yalu River. China regarded this border breach as a threat and sent the Chinese People's Volunteer Army into North Korea in October. With the support of the Chinese, the KPA forced the UN contingent back into South Korea. By 1951 the war had become a series of advancements and retreats that hovered around the 38th parallel and exacted a heavy toll on soldiers and civilians on both sides. By July, negotiations for an armistice were already underway.

On July 27, 1953, all military hostilities between the North and South ceased with the signing of Korean Armistice Agreement, though technically the war never officially ended—there has never been a declaration of peace. The warring sides agreed to a military demarcation line at the 38th parallel. This line would be demilitarized, a condition to be enforced indefinitely by a Military Armistice Commission. The armistice, though not explicitly a peace treaty, effectively put a stop to the bloodshed. However, a lot of blood had already been spilled, and the damage was irreparable: The Korean War took roughly 2 million civilian lives, and no progress was made toward Korean unification. The Korean War was a cataclysmic illustration of willpower and stubbornness, a regional conflict galvanized by the Cold War, a war by proxy between the United States and the Soviet Union.

THE BEGINNING OF THE KIMS

FROM THE ASHES OF THE KOREAN WAR, A DESPOT RISES

For North Koreans, induction to the cult of personality begins on the first day of nursery school. They are introduced to their leader through a fictitious story mirroring the birth of Kim Il-sung, on April 15, 1912, with the birth of the universe. Following the creation of the universe, Il-Sung has forever ruled the Democratic People's Republic of Korea as Eternal President. His many sacrifices for Korea entitle him to complete authority over the Democratic People's Republic, even from his final resting place at the Kumsusan Palace of the Sun, also known as Kumsusan Memorial Palace.

Under the government of North Korea, worship of the godlike Kim Il-sung is demanded. There is no debate, and contesting this imperative of worship carries a severe consequence: imprisonment in a gulag-style labor camp. The few who have emerged or

Left: Mansudae Hill, Pyongyang: the 66-foot-tall bronze statue of the Great Leader Kim Il-sung

escaped from these camps describe extreme physical mistreatment and human rights violations.

Kim Il-sung secured himself the position of Eternal President early in his regime. Within his first few years in office, he purged political rivals within the Korean Workers' Party (KWP) through executions and labor camp sentences. Being the unopposed leader allowed him to stall the signing of the armistice agreement to end the Korean War. As the war dragged on, the incessant bombing by the American-led United Nations Command and the resulting death, famine, and demolition of infrastructure served as fodder for a massive propaganda campaign against the West.

The KWP had suffered great losses in the war, and Kim Il-sung responded to this by creating a party of peasants and manual laborers easy to manipulate. This underprivileged class was war-weary and vulnerable to anyone who would uplift them, and, understanding this inherent vulnerability, Kim Il-sung invited them to enlist in the KWP, where they would be rewarded for their loyalty. Many of these impoverished Koreans were keenly thrilled to have the recognition of the all-knowing Il-sung, especially after years of suffering from the gripping chokehold of destitution, hunger, and homelessness. Recognition from the Eternal President was essentially a dream come true to them, and they henceforth showed complete loyalty to Il-sung and the KWP.

By 1953, the KWP mushroomed into a 450,000-member organization of war-hardened communist peasants, ready to rebuild postwar North Korea in Kim Il-sung's image. In their eyes, Il-sung was a shimmering beacon of light; he provided them with jobs, housing, and food in proportion to their party loyalty. Life was hard for the citizens, who worked long hours making weapons to secure the new state, but they were told that an age of prosperity was soon approaching and that their sacrifices would liberate North Korea from imperialism once and for all.

KIM IMPOSES AN ISOLATIONIST PHILOSOPHY

Although Kim Il-sung feigned a lack of interest in foreign politics, he was not pleased with the new Soviet administration, led by Nikita Khrushchev, who was leaning toward peace with the West. Khrushchev scorned Stalinism as a dangerous cult of personality that used terrorism as its primary method of effecting change, a distressing signal to Il-sung that his relationship with the Soviet Union was dissipating. Severing ties with the Soviet Union, however, posed a major problem. Il-sung, who peddled isolationist rhetoric to the North Korean populace, had clandestinely relied on Soviet support for critical aid. He delivered a speech before North Korean propagandists and agitators on December 28, 1955, titled "On Eliminating Dogmatism and Formalism and Establishing Juche in Ideological Work," in which he introduced the concept of *juche* or "self-reliance and subjectivity."

Juche is a Korean isolationist policy whereby domestic self-reliance obviates the need for international relations of any kind. Although juche is an adaptation of Marxism-Leninism, Confucianism underlies its basic philosophy. Under juche, Kim Il-sung is regarded as a benevolent, omnipresent, and omniscient "father figure," and the people of North Korea, the "children" in this analogy, face consequences for disobedience, and rewards—food and shelter—for obedience.

Under the juche policy, artists and writers were charged with promoting Kim Il-sung's image as *suryong* or "Great Leader." In paintings, the Great Leader was portrayed as a father figure with

SUN-DAY

Kim Il-sung's birthday on April 15 is a national holiday in North Korea, known as the Day of Sun. North Koreans are required to celebrate it by worshipping at statues of Il-sung and renewing their oaths of loyalty to him. Although he died in 1994, fireworks still lit up the sky over Pyongyang on April 15, 2015, and Kim Jong-un, his grandson, led the official occasion at his mausoleum.

masses of obedient Koreans looking to him for wisdom. Similarly, North Korean literature emphasized the plights and joys of socialism, generating a feeling of pride in readers and reenergizing them for the great struggle. North Korean literature was also the vehicle through which the "real" history of the world would be told. In this fictitious history, the cosmos burst forth at the moment of Il-sung's birth. While Il-sung's visions of grandeur were megalomaniacal, loyalty to the regime was the only form of cultural currency in North Korea, and hence accepting this history, or at least remaining silent about one's doubts, was the only way to survive.

Despite having ordered his personal doctors to find a way for him to live to be 120 years old, Kim Il-sung died at the age of 84 on July 8, 1994, and was succeeded by his son, Kim Jong-il. Waves of weeping citizens were witnessed throughout North Korea, and some of them were incontrovertibly participating in public mourning under the threat of death or imprisonment. The Eternal President had made every effort to live longer, including establishing a research center in Pyongyang for doctors to discover ways to prolong his life; one method they devised was to supply him with blood

Wall mural of Kim Il-sung, at the Victorious Fatherland Liberation War Museum, Pyongyang

transfusions from young men. Il-sung lies embalmed in a glass case at the Kumsusan Palace of the Sun, where he is covered from the neck down by the KWP flag.

Between 1949 and 1992, roughly 40,000 statues and busts of Kim Il-sung were made. Artistic renderings of his image are revered with a sweeping religious fervor and, in public, they are venerated with the utmost respect. In private, every home is supposed to carry a likeness of the Great Leader and treat the image as if it were Il-sung himself. Although his son and his grandson succeeded him as leaders of North Korea, no one is capable of surpassing him under the juche philosophy. After all, how can he have any contenders after, according to the rhetoric, creating the world, defeating Japan in World War II, winning the Korean War in three days, and crushing American imperialism?

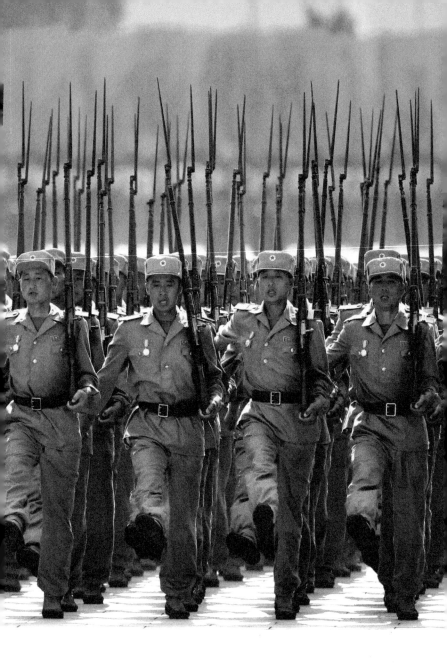

JUCHE

STALINISM INSPIRES, CONTRASTS WITH NORTH KOREAN ISOLATIONISM IN THE *JUCHE* STATE POLICY

IN North Korea, the juche state policy includes four basic tenets: (1) Man controls his own destiny; (2) The people are the masters of the revolution; (3) The revolution must be carried out in a "self-reliant" manner; (4) The "secret weapon" of the revolution is complete loyalty to the Great Leader.

Juche ideology is rooted in Marxism and Stalinism. Like Stalinism, it offers a central "father figure" for the people to revere and obey, where Kim Il-sung replaces Stalin at the center of the cult of personality, and, like Marxism, it emphasizes collectivism and working toward a common goal. However, juche differs in its explicit focus on Korean values, specifically Confucianism, and in its goal for unification with the South. Juche emphasizes the notion that Korea is a "chosen land" and that Koreans are the most privileged of all races. It differs from Marxism in that it idealizes Korean statehood as a kind of communist Shangri-La. Marxism, by contrast, looks forward to a time when man will break free from statehood and live unencumbered by government.

Left: North Korean soldiers carrying guns march to mark the 60th anniversary of the signing of a truce in the 1950–1953 Korean War at Kim Il-sung Square, in Pyongyang, July 27, 2013.

SON OF
THE SUN

KIM JONG-IL LEAVES A LEGACY
OF DESTRUCTION AND DESPAIR

The Korean War and postwar years left the Korean peninsula territorially, economically, and socially divided. Although both North and South Korea suffered great losses of life and infrastructure, their recovery strategies served to shape them into the nations they are today. In South Korea, the adoption of

Above: Eternal President Kim Il-sung shows the way to his son Kim Jong-il, his successor as Supreme Leader of North Korea, in this fresco at the Wonsan University of Agriculture.

democratic elections and capitalist economic policies created a globalized economy. Meanwhile, the rise of Kim Il-sung's cult of personality in North Korea created an autocracy where socio-economic policies primarily serve to venerate Il-sung and his successors. Il-sung's seat of supreme leadership of the Democratic People's Republic of Korea was therefore hotly contested among potential male heirs. The prospective successors included Il-sung's younger brother (Kim Yong-ju), his stepbrother (Kim P'yong-il), and his son (Kim Jong-il).

In the autocratic environment of North Korea, nepotism and fawning over the current leader were highly rewarded. Kim Jong-il understood this, so he demonstrated his devotion to his father through larger-than-life film productions, artistic monuments, and works of literature. A few years after his graduation from Kim Il-sung University in 1963, he joined the Korean Workers' Party, and in 1968 became head of the department of Propaganda and Agitation. With this authority, Jong-il formed the 4-15 Creation Group, so named to commemorate his father's birthday on April 15. As a government agency, its sole mission was to erect statues and monuments of Il-sung throughout the country. By 1992, with the North Korean populace suffering one of the worst famines in history, 40,000 statues of Il-sung had been erected.

Moreover, Kim Jong-il poured the bulk of his artistic efforts into propaganda film production. He opened seven production studios in North Korea and conscripted actors and filmmakers throughout the country—he even kidnapped some from South Korea and brought them to Pyongyang—to produce over 8,000 propaganda films. The most significant of his films were remakes of popular movies, such as the American *Gone with the Wind*. The plots were altered to focus on his father and appeal to the supposed revolutionary sentiment of all North Koreans.

FACT-FINDING

Official North Korean history says Kim Jong-il was born on the sacred Mount Paektu (above) on February 16, 1942. In truth, however, Jong-il was actually born in Siberia a year earlier under the name Yuri Irsenovich Kim. Although the official biography doesn't explicitly say so, Jong-il probably spent the duration of the Korean War period in the relative safety of remote Manchuria.

A SUCCESSOR STEPS UP

Kim Jong-il's movies were deeply rooted in anti-Americanism, and citizens were forced to watch and discuss them as a form of state-mandated education. Kim Il-sung took pride in the films, both as the "muse" and the father of the filmmaker. Having curried sufficient favor with his father, Jong-il was anointed as his father's successor in 1974. To distinguish him, Jong-il was given the title "Dear Leader." At once, Il-sung no longer had to worry about succession. Over the ensuing 20 years until Il-sung's death on July 8, 1994, Jong-il took on increasing levels of responsibility.

Although Kim Jong-il had secured his position as the next leader of North Korea, he paled in comparison to his father. He lacked the military training, physical characteristics, and personality traits that allowed the Supreme Leader to maintain his omnipresence in the cultural life of the country. Whereas Kim Il-sung was tall, broad-shouldered, and fairly convivial in public appearances, Jong-il was short, squat, and somewhat uncomfortable in social settings. Even more pressing was the fact that, unlike Il-sung, Jong-il was not a revolutionary. He had a relatively cushioned childhood, since his father's status as major of the first battalion of the 88th Red Army Brigade afforded his family a decent home in Siberia. This distinction made the public wary of him, as he seemed too spoiled and pampered to lead a nation whose political hierarchal structure would render him their national "father."

To strengthen the legitimacy of his impending rule, Kim Jong-il committed acts of terror. According to North Korean defector Hwang Jang-yop, former Chairman of the North Korean Supreme People's Assembly, Jong-il was responsible for the attempted assassination of South Korean president Chun Doo-hwan in 1983, the bombing at Gimpo International Airport in 1986, and the bombing of Korean Air civilian flight 858 in 1987. As a member of the Politburo, the most powerful and influential subsection of the Korean Workers' Party, Jong-il further antagonized world leaders by acting in defiance of the Nuclear Non-Proliferation Treaty, an international agreement to cease the development of nuclear weapons. Although Kim Il-sung signed the agreement in 1985, North Korea quickly went on to build the Yongbyon Nuclear Scientific Research Center, where scientists worked to produce fuel for nuclear reactors.

The leadership of Il-sung overlapped somewhat with that of Jong-Il, as the younger Kim worked to establish himself. Events in South Korea further incited Kim Il-sung's interest in nuclear weapons. Against the South's modern, globalizing economy, the North's dwindling food rations, constant electric outages, and limited supply of consumer goods suggested a socioeconomic crisis north of the 38th parallel. When the 1988 Olympics were hosted in Seoul, this event flew in the face of every piece of North Korean political propaganda about the South being inferior to the North.

Additionally, Kim Il-sung invested in massive projects to demonstrate North Korea's wealth, with each of them, however, funded by foreign loans. These projects included hosting the World Festival of

Youth and Students for an "Olympic-type event" in Pyongyang, the West Sea Barrage to build the longest dam in the world, and the massive tideland reclamation project to irrigate coastal land. None of these projects were completed. North Korea's massive spending campaign to stroke Il-sung's ego arrived at a particularly bad time with the fall of the Soviet Union in 1991.

The collapse of the Soviet Union brought about the end of North Korea's main source of financial support. From the end of the Korean War until the late 1980s, the Soviet Union had regularly supplied North Korea with aid. While this money could have been used on agriculture and trade agreements with other nations, it was instead poured into the military, in accordance with the songun philosophy. Scud missiles, submarines, and fleets of

expensive fighter jets were prioritized over the basic needs of the North Korean populace. To bolster its food supplies, North Korea looked to China, but political alliances dictated the liquidation of this aid. Perhaps the worst blow, however, was that, unlike the Soviet Union, Russia would not give North Korea discounted prices on oil. North Korea was therefore unable to acquire the energy necessary to function at even the minimum level of production.

ECONOMIC COLLAPSE

Between 1987 and 1990, crude oil imports to North Korea dropped from 22 percent to 7 percent. This forced North Koreans to burn

Painting in the Korean Art Museum of leader
Kim Jong-il visiting his troops

wood for fuel, leading to massive deforestation. With the land effectively stripped, Korea's otherwise normal monsoon season led to catastrophic flooding in 1995 and 1996. Much of North Korea's hydroelectric power was destroyed, the coal industry was shut down, and the last remaining crops were decimated: 70 percent of the annual rice harvest, 50 percent of the maize harvest, and 988,000 acres of arable land. The floods laid waste to 3 million tons of emergency grains, destroyed bridges, hospitals, rail systems, and roads, and left swaths of people homeless. The economy was in free fall, and the population began to starve. Amid such losses, social connections deteriorated. North Korean defectors recount the horrors of mass starvation: people eating grasses and tree bark for sustenance, entire families committing suicide together, and children digging through animal dung for pieces of corn.

Roughly 1 million North Korean people died of starvation and starvation-related illnesses between 1995 and 1998.

In response, the government issued a statement that the monsoons, which disproportionately affected the poor rural region of Hwanghae, were nothing out of the ordinary and that the government's economic management was certainly not to blame. North Korean leaders proceeded to impose strict rules for "unbecoming" behavior during the famine. Executions were carried out for theft, slaughtering animals for food, and public urination. A "Let's Eat Two Meals Per Day" campaign was launched to inspire everyone to work harder and eat less, though North Korea received a total of $2.3 billion from the United Nations, South Korea, and non-governmental organizations in the 1990s. Food donations from the United States, South Korea, Japan, and China provided 80 percent of all food consumed in North Korea between 1997 and 2007.

With massive food donations from foreign nations, Kim Jong-il gave himself carte blanche to devote the $2.3 billion cash donation to military projects in his new songun or "military first" policy. Under songun, Jong-il transferred the power of the Korean Workers' Party to the National Defense Commission and appointed himself as the chairman. He summarily transformed North Korean culture into military culture, blurring the lines between civilians and soldiers with a compulsory 10 years of military service for men. As of 2015, women are required to serve three

{ **Chollima** A North Korean economics policy arguing that a nation's economic shortcomings can be fixed if industry workers put in maximal effort. }

DID YOU KNOW

The Korean Central News Agency is the only news station in North Korea. Its rhetorical reporting style describes the United States as an "imperialist warmonger." In one deriding denouncement, former US Secretary of Defense Donald Rumsfeld was called a "fascist tyrant who puts an ogre to shame."

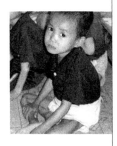

LOYALTY LOTTO

Food in North Korea is allotted according to a public distribution system based on entitlement: age, occupation, and, most importantly, party loyalty are the factors that establish entitlement. According to this system, children receive the least allotment of food. In 2011, US nongovernmental organizations in North Korea found 7-year-olds weighing 15 pounds in rural areas outside Pyongyang.

years. To Jong-il, it seemed a logical step to pour all the nation's resources into the common goal of defense. As a result, North Korea is completely dependent on foreign food donations, but it is one of the most militarized countries on Earth.

Roughly 1 million North Korean people died of starvation and starvation-related illnesses between 1995 and 1998. The infant mortality rate increased by more than 25 percent between 1993 and 1997, and in 1998 the World Food Programme found that the prevalence of stunted growth due to malnutrition was more than 60 percent. All the while, Kim Jong-il continued to treat himself to lavish gifts in the capital. Disturbing statistics from the height of the famine reveal that he spent $2.6 million on Swiss watches, millions on a US professional wrestling exhibition in 1995, and $20 million on 200 new Mercedes-Benz limousines in 1998. Jong-il also hosted a "joy brigade" of women who were forced to "entertain" him at his will. He sent his personal chef on international shopping sprees for the finest Italian cheeses and Japanese fish, and he was, until his death, an avid consumer of Hennessy Paradis cognac.

{ **Kkot chebi** The children who were orphaned or abandoned during the North Korean famine of the 1990s. The literal translation is "flowering swallows." }

A propaganda picture of North Korea's reclusive leader Kim Jong-il posed in a field of grain. Since a state of famine was declared in the isolated state in the late 1990s, some estimates project that as many as 2 million people have died of starvation.

Kim Jong-il's luxury expenditures during the flood and famine that afflicted North Korea reflect the infantile nature of his leadership. Up until his death on December 19, 2011, he pampered and spoiled himself at the expense of his nation. Jong-il used his immense power and wealth for attaining personal goals, whether it was developing nuclear weapons or enjoying the finest food. His true legacy, however, consists of the poverty and oppression he imposed on North Korea, with a toll that will reverberate long after his death.

THE
DMZ

THE MOST HEAVILY MONITORED BORDER HAS A LIFE OF ITS OWN

A wide swath across the Korean Peninsula boasts high-voltage wire fences that surround 2 million soldiers, 1 million land-mines, and the occasional Amur Leopard. About 160 miles from west to east and 2.5 miles wide, the Demilitarized Zone (DMZ) at the North-South Korean border is one of the lasting legacies of the Cold War. At the end of the Korean War in 1953, neither country recognized the other's legitimacy. The establishment of

North Korean soldiers look south through binoculars during a visit by Korean War veterans to the truce village of Panmunjom in the demilitarised zone separating the two Koreas in Paju, about 34 miles north of Seoul and 130 miles south of the North Korean capital of Pyongyang.

the DMZ was not a peace treaty—an important distinction taken seriously by both sides—but it effectively stopped the fighting and has, despite occasional incursions, prevented a second full-out war from breaking out. The July 27, 1953 armistice identified the latitudinal line at 38° 0´ N as the de facto border, since this is where the warring armies were at the time of its signing. According to the agreement, a Military Armistice Commission would enforce the border until a "lasting peace" could be achieved. In the meantime, nature has flourished.

Representatives of the UN Command Military Armistice Commission as well as North and South Korea attend a meeting in the Military Armistice Building. The building is constructed directly over the line of demarcation between the two countries, as indicated by the microphone cords on the table.

The DMZ is divided by the Military Demarcation Line, beyond which neither side can legally pass. The DMZ crosses the Korean Peninsula at 38° 0′ N on a slight angle, so that the west side lies south of the latitudinal line and the east side lies north of it. West of the peninsula, in the Yellow Sea, the Northern Limit Line is the maritime border, but it does not define the border as well as the DMZ does on land, and skirmishes over crabbing and fishing sometimes occur.

Located in the abandoned village of Panmunjon on the far western edge of the border, the Joint Security Area is the only place where North and South Korean soldiers meet face-to-face. Meetings are held in the Conference Row buildings, which are crossed by the Military Demarcation Line. Photographs show a purposely drawn black line evenly dividing the conference desks. During meetings, North and South Korean officials bring flags, which they affix to desk stands and place antagonistically close to the line. Directly to the north of Conference Row is Panmun Hall, where Korean Workers' Party officials work. To the south is Freedom House, where South Korea hopes to reunite families separated by the war.

Panmunjon is directly outside of the Conference Row buildings, and this is where guards from either side stand as they have since 1953. North and South Korean governments assign only the most intimidating men to this task. South Korean troops designated for border duty must be at least 5-foot-8, while North Korean troops are selected based on who appears the best fed. An official stare-down takes place between two units outside of Conference Row, where the South looks head-on at the North. By contrast, two Northern guards face each other while one stands facing North Korea. They are arranged this way so as to discourage defecting. This speaks to the notion that the most "entitled" men in the country might defect if they did not fear being killed instantly by guards at Panmun Hall.

Despite these defensive measures, incursions over the DMZ have occurred from time to time. Throughout the late 1960s, border

skirmishes were so frequent that they were collectively referred to as the Second Korean War, or the Korean DMZ Conflict. Kim Il-sung initiated the conflict with a 1966 speech to the Korean Workers' Party about creating a division between South Korea and the United States through "irregular warfare." He wanted to target American troops and force them to leave the South's side. This, he believed, would make South Korea vulnerable to insurgencies and invasion. Il-sung's first offensive strike was a November 2, 1966, ambush on a South Korean Army patrol squad. The South was taken off guard, and eight

officers were killed. Such ambushes became commonplace over the ensuing three years, and included the capture of the USS *Pueblo*, a Navy intelligence ship in the East China Sea. By the time the fighting had ended in 1969, nearly 400 North Korean soldiers had died—more than American and South Korean soldiers combined.

Below: A South Korean soldier exits the Second Tunnel, an "infiltration" tunnel dug by North Korea, near the Demilitarized Zone (DMZ) in Cheorwon, South Korea.

BREAK-DOWN ACROSS THE BORDERS

NORTH KOREA

military:
1.2
million

population:
25
million

DMZ

SOUTH KOREA

military:
0.7
million

population:
50
million

The population and military service numbers of North and South Korea are nearly perfect inversions of each other. The South has twice as many people in total, while the North has twice as many serving in the military.

Values are approximate

NATURE FLOURISHES

Despite the ongoing power struggle around the DMZ border, an abundance of wildlife has flourished. Endangered species of plants and animals inhabit the area, including the Amur Leopard, which would have become extinct from poaching had it not been for the human-free DMZ. A 2009 ecology report by the Korean "Tigerman" Lim Sun Nam found 70 kinds of mammals, 320 kinds of birds, and 2,000 species of plants living along the DMZ. This great biodiversity exists along the DMZ thanks to the diversity of the terrain itself. The DMZ crosses through prairies, mountains, lakes, tidal marshes, and swamps.

South Korea attempted to protect the area's wildlife by applying for a United Nations Environmental, Scientific, and Cultural Organization (UNESCO) designation for its side of the DMZ. The South formally requested that Pyongyang push for its own designation in 2011. The North instead asked UNESCO to deny South Korea's request because it would violate the 1953 armistice. North Korea threw its considerable weight around the UNESCO office in Paris, using its membership status at the international coordinating council to influence the decision. In the summer of 2012, Pyongyang issued letters to every UNESCO council member with typical North Korean rhetoric about the South's ulterior motives for the designation request, and the North was successful: On July 12 the South was denied protection for wildlife on its side of the DMZ.

OVER THE
DMZ BORDER

The lush natural beauty of the DMZ is deceptively peaceful. Both sides have made incursions across the line, which keeps the atmosphere tense, even amidst nature's tranquility.

August 18, 1976 North Korean soldiers at the Joint Security Area killed two American soldiers who were cutting down a tree on the South side of the Military Demarcation Line. The tree had been blocking the Americans' view of the North. Upon seeing them at work, North Korean soldiers rushed across the border and beat the Americans to death with the blunt side of their own axes. Days later, accompanied by a small armada of helicopters, South Korean soldiers brought the tree down in Operation Paul Bunyan, showing the North they would not be intimidated.

July 14, 1977 An American CH-47 Chinook helicopter strayed into North Korean airspace and was shot down. Only one of the four airmen survived. He was temporarily detained in a North Korean prison.

December 17, 1994 Another American helicopter flew into North Korea. The OH-58A Kiowa was shot down, killing two of the airmen on board. One survived and was imprisoned for 13 days.

July 16, 1997 A 30-minute gunfire exchange raged over the border after 14 members of the Korean People's Army crossed the Military Demarcation Line.

May 26, 2006 The South fired warning shots after two North Korean soldiers ventured dangerously close to the Military Demarcation Line.

October 6, 2012 A teenage private of the Korean People's Army knocked on the South Korean barracks at the Freedom House to defect. He had recently killed two of his superiors in order to escape the regime.

A POWERLESS COUNTRY

RHETORIC ALONE WILL NEVER BRING LIGHT TO THE SUBJECT OF NORTH KOREA'S DARKNESS

IN 2014 NASA released a satellite photo of the Korean peninsula at night. Without a caption, however, the real importance of the photo may not be fully understood. The illuminated outlines of China and South Korea are apparent in the photo, but a conspicuous darkness between them makes it difficult to see that the vacuum of blackness itself is North Korea.

The only telltale sign of civilization in the photo is a tiny speck of light in the region of Pyongyang, where the illuminated Juche Tower is plugged in to power sources around-the-clock. Otherwise, the bankrupt regime cannot afford to provide electricity to the nation.

Energy shortages have been commonplace in North Korea since the collapse of the Soviet Union, when aid to the North was suddenly halted. A devastating famine and flood followed, and a restrictive economic policy never allowed the nation to regain its footing. In 2015 each person in North Korea used 739 watts of electric power per year; by contrast, individuals in the South used 10,162.

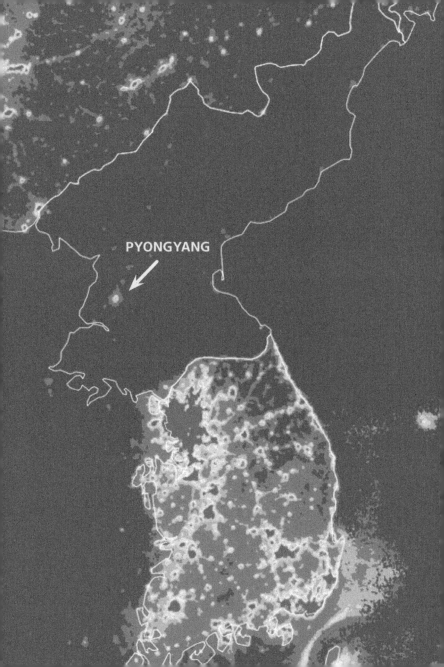

THE TOP 10

THE KIMS' MOST FAR-FETCHED CLAIMS

1 **The world began** on April 15, 1912, the day Great Leader Kim Il-sung was born. In 1997 Kim Jong-il abandoned the Western calendar in favor of the new juche calendar, where the year "1" corresponds to the year 1912.

2 **In World War II,** Kim Il-sung defeated Japan with a single guerilla army of Korean rebel fighters. He went on to head the North Korean army in the three-day-long Korean War, instigated by the South.

3 **When it comes to golfing,** nobody could out-do Kim Jong-il, who made 11 holes-in-one on his first attempt at golfing.

4 **A star and double rainbow** appeared in the sky at the moment of Kim Jong-il's birth.

5 **When he was three weeks old,** Kim Jong-il began walking. He was speaking in full sentences at eight weeks. Later into his childhood he learned how to control the weather with his thoughts.

6 **Kim Jong-il** never used toilets because he did not defecate. The Dear Leader's body had apparently evolved beyond digestion.

7 **Hamburgers** were invented by Kim Jong-il. This was first reported in the North Korean media outlet Minju Joson, stating that Jong-il had invented the "double bread with meat." Factories were made to manufacture the new sandwiches for university students.

8 **As a college student,** Kim Jong-il wrote 1,500 books during his three-year stay at Kim Il-sung University.

9 **A swallow** foretold the miraculous birth of the Dear Leader Kim Jong-il on the sacred Mount Paektu, the birthplace of the Korean people.

10 **Kim Jong-un** claims that North Korea has developed a ginseng-based drug that can cure AIDS, Ebola, and cancer.

FAN(ATIC)

HOW THE KIMS USE FILM FOR INDOCTRINATION

From its beginning as a divided state, North Korea has used film as propaganda, as a method of communicating political ideas. The People's Film Society was established as the Soviets arrived in 1945 for the express purpose of showing Soviet films to North Koreans. Kim Il-sung, rising as the nation's first leader, immediately noted that film was more efficient in delivering the communist message than any other form of media. In 1947, Il-sung helped found the first North Korean film studio, the Korea Feature Film Studio. Over the next two years, the Soviet Union gradually turned filmmaking authority over to North Korea.

During this time, the first North Korean film, *Nae Kohyang* ("My Hometown," 1949) was released. *Nae Kohyang* idealized the simplicity and innocence of peasantry against the mountainous setting of rural Korea. It spoke to the joy of Korean liberation from Japan and stretched the truth as needed to put Kim Il-sung at the head of the liberation front. *Nae Kohyang* fulfilled its purpose of moving viewers with the idea that their new and long-awaited independence was entirely Il-sung's doing.

Facilitated by the effectiveness and efficiency of film, the cult of personality surrounding Kim Il-sung and his successors

Left: An undated portrait of former North Korean leader Kim Jong-il

progressively flourished after the Korean War. Aware of the war-weary North Korean populace's vulnerability, Il-sung launched artistic campaigns to persuade them that he was a demigod worthy of their homage. Film was one of Il-sung's favorite methods of indoctrination, and with the help of the Soviet Union, North Korean film culture became the country's greatest form of propaganda.

Although Kim Il-sung had long believed in film as a way to "rally support" for the regime, it was his son, Kim Jong-il, who took North Korean film culture to a whole new level. After he graduated from Kim Il-sung University in 1963, Jong-il took a primary interest in producing films. He also wanted to win his father's approval as heir. During a short prison sentence in China, Il-sung had conceived the ideas for Jong-il's first films, *Sea of Blood* (1969) and *Flower Girl* (1972). The plots centered on Korean girls whose attempts at living happy and healthy lives were undercut by Japanese racism in 1930s Korea.

Kim Il-sung loved *Sea of Blood* and *Flower Girl*, and Kim Jong-il's book *On the Art of the Cinema* (1973) brought him into the North Korean pop culture limelight. The book glorified the socialist-nationalist juche ideology and introduced the "seed theory" of North Korean juche art and cinema. Jong-il asserts that all forms of art are rooted in a single ideology, the "seed." When it comes to filmmaking, the entire production team must work toward

---

North Korea and the Soviet Union signed a cultural exchange agreement in 1949. As North Korea sent its movies and dance troupes to Moscow, the Soviet Union sent its literature to North Korea. With the arrival of the Soviet Union's literature and the accessibility of it to the North Korean populace, Russian became North Korea's official second language.

In this March 1979 photo from North Korea's official Korean Central News Agency, distributed by Korea News Service, leader Kim Jong-il gives advice at the shooting of *An Jung Geun Avenges Hirobumi Ito,* a narrative film.

"sprouting" the single seed. A director must, therefore, keep foreign ideas from entering the team's collective consciousness. Seed theory, Jong-il believed, would lend itself well to North Korean cinema as propaganda. In his book, he explains how the seed of cinema in North Korea would be the exaltation of the leadership of the regime.

On the Art of the Cinema might have helped Kim Jong-il secure his position with his father—who anointed him successor a

ART IMITATES ART

Australian director Anna Broinowski applied Kim Jong-il's filmmaking principles from On the Art of the Cinema *to her movie,* Aim High in Creation!, *a film about making North Korean propaganda films.*

year after the book's publication—but it did not advance North Korean film production in any significant way. The book targeted an audience of international professional filmmakers, but they did not find it enlightening, and they noted no artistic or production differences between the films made before and after its publication. Jong-il, frustrated by this lack of acknowledgment, went on to kidnap South Korean filmmaker Shin Sang-ok and his ex-wife, actress Choi Eun-hee, in 1978. Until their escape from North Korea in 1986, the former couple was forced to make seven films for the regime and give complete filmmaking credit to Jong-il. Among these films was *Pulgasari* (1985), which personified capitalism as a monster devouring the collectivist Korean people.

Using the film industry as a propaganda machine is common in autocracies like North Korea. Kim Il-sung and Kim Jong-il adopted this strategy from Soviet leaders Vladimir Lenin and Joseph Stalin, who understood that emotions and belief systems could be manipulated through cinema and visual storytelling. However, while the Soviets provided the idea of film as a powerful tool of mass manipulation, Jong-il rejected the sullen Soviet filmmaking style in favor of the more glamorous and grandiose American style. Jong-il himself was a huge fan of Elizabeth Taylor and Sean Connery. He adored *Gone With the Wind* (1936), *Rambo* (1985), *Friday the 13th* (1980), and the James Bond series, and his personal library boasted up to 20,000 films.

Despite the starvation and economic ruin prevalent in the world of North Korean peasants, Kim Jong-il proceeded to glorify their lives on screen, believing that filmmaking was of the utmost importance in keeping spirits high in the face of these challenges. "Film is a most popular and mobile art," he said in 1992. "[It] can be shown to a large number of people anytime, anywhere, in a short time.... Anyone can easily understand it." Jong-il believed the mobility of film would allow it to reach and affect the poor people outside of Pyongyang, where 3 to 5 percent of the population died from starvation, starvation-related illnesses, and flooding during the 1990s. Throughout his life and leadership, Jong-il responded to criticism about being out of touch with his impoverished citizenry with finely crafted North Korean rhetoric that blamed social ills on South Korea and the United States.

The significance of cinema to the North Korean propaganda machine is evidenced in education and "reeducation" policies that require students and teachers to view specific films. School-age children compete in nationwide contests by reciting lengthy film passages, and college-age film and literature students are required to read *On the Art of the Cinema*. Through film, Kim Jong-il vied to make a "juche man" out of every Korean: a person who would think, speak, and work in lockstep with the regime.

KIM JONG-UN TAKES CONTROL

THE MOST MYSTERIOUS OF LEADERS

How does the third-generation leader of North Korea stack up against both his father and grandfather? In a culture where actual worship of his predecessor is mandatory, is it even possible for Kim Jong-un to distinguish himself? There might not be any other head of state on the planet about whom more is speculated—and less is actually known.

The camouflaging of the details of Kim Jong-un's life starts at the beginning: The year of his birth is a matter of debate. He might

Above: Kim Jong-un inspects a live ammunition firing drill by the Jangjae Islet Defense Detachment and the Mu Islet Hero Defense Detachment.

have been born in 1983 or 1984, but the official party line is that he joined the Kim family in 1982, 70 years after the moment of his grandfather's birth—according to the state-sanctioned history. Jong-un's mother, Ko Young Hui, a dancer, was allegedly the most important woman in Kim Jong-il's life, surpassing his wife and three other known mistresses. Jong-un attended boarding school in Switzerland and then returned to North Korea for college. During his youth, his ascendency to leadership of the country wasn't a foregone conclusion; in fact, his older brother, Kim Jong-nam, was first in line for the role before a faux pas involving a trip to Disneyland on a fake passport suddenly derailed him. Beginning in roughly 2009, Jong-il made the decision to pass power to Jong-un and started to establish his son among the country's leadership, dubbing him a four-star general and making more concerted media appearances together. By the time Jong-il passed away in 2011, Jong-un's installation as his successor was already complete.

In the legacy of the Kim Dynasty, Kim Jong-un's place is anything but cemented. Aside from the basic biographic information about him (Jong-un married Ri Sol Ju at some point between 2009 and 2011, and

DEATH, NOTICED

The international press can be a little too eager in its coverage of North Korea's high-profile deaths. Despite speculation and reports that Kim Jong-un had his ex-girlfriend executed, for example, the rumors of her death turned out to be greatly exaggerated. Hyon Song Wol, a singer who was allegedly killed by firing squad in 2013, was seen very much alive during a television interview in 2014.

they have a daughter who was born in 2012), the majority of what's known about Jong-un is open to interpretation. He famously dismissed his uncle Jang Sung-taek in 2013 for being disloyal to the party—and dismissal from government in North Korea means execution. The fact of Jang's death cannot be disputed, but the motivations behind it can be. Was this a power move by Jong-un aimed at establishing himself not only as an heir to the throne, but as a shrewd and powerful dictator in his own right? Was it a scare tactic to alert the members of his government that no one was beyond the scope of his retribution for disloyalty, including family members? Or was it in fact indicative of Jong-un's status as a figurehead, orchestrated by the Korean Workers' Party Organization and Guidance Department, a group established by Kim Jong-il in the 1990s and rumored to be the actual seat of power within the country? Depending on the defector or political analyst being interviewed, any of these possibilities is likely.

As was true of his father and grandfather before him, Kim Jong-un exists in a swirling whirlpool of outlandish claims and actions that have severe domestic and international consequences. For one, there's the 2013 *VICE Guide to North Korea*, a documentary made when the magazine arranged for Dennis Rodman and three of the Harlem Globetrotters to visit Pyongyang and party with Jong-un. Contrast the image of Jong-un and Rodman courtside with an announcement of a successful nuclear test in the same year. Like so many other facets of Jong-un's leadership, the details of the test and how North Korea's nuclear capabilities ultimately affect the international community are still—purposefully—unclear.

KIM & FRIENDS

AN AMERICAN BASKETBALL PLAYER, A SPANISH ARISTOCRAT, AND A HONG KONG BANKER

Dennis Rodman, once famous for wearing the number 91 Chicago Bulls jersey, first traveled to North Korea in 2013. He quickly became "best friends" with the despot and sang him "Happy Birthday" in Pyongyang in January 2014. "To see a guy like that, this 5-foot-2 or 5-foot-1 guy, have that much power, in a country like that, and see people get emotional, crying, 20,000 of them clapping, it was so surreal. It blew my mind," he told *The Hollywood Reporter* in January 2015.

Alejandro Cao de Benos is another friend of the Kims. The Spanish aristocrat established the Korean Friendship Association because he was attracted to the North Korean values of discipline and honor. Benos's mission is to promote the Kim regime to the entire world.

Hong Kong businessman Johnny Hon is on a similar mission with the International Kim Il-sung Foundation, which is intended to spread the juche ideology worldwide. Hon created the foundation in 2012 after Kim Jong-il rejected his takeover of Daedong Credit Bank in Pyongyang.

BALLOONING REVOLUTION

Though it might not immediately seem like the first course of action for an act of revolution against a totalitarian regime, sending weather balloons from South Korea into North Korea has become one of the more popular methods of anti-Kim activism. North Korean defectors now living in the South have sent thousands of balloons carrying bundles of leaflets, pamphlets, and flash drives loaded with contraband entertainment. The hope is that by exposing North Koreans to entertainment from the outside world, the activists will be able to crack the societal norm of the Kim propaganda machine. Here are a few of the emissary shows and movies that have been dropped across the borders: *Lucy, Son of God, 22 Jump Street, Friends, The Interview, Titanic, Pretty Woman, Desperate Housewives, Snowpiercer,* and *The Great Dictator.*

Left: North Korean defectors release balloons carrying anti–North Korea leaflets at Imjingak Peace Park in Paju near the Demilitarized Zone (DMZ) on April 15, 2012. The Korean banner reads "Let's terminate Kim Jong-un's dictatorship!"

ENEMIES OF THE STATE

THE GULAGS OVERFLOW WITH POLITICAL PRISONERS AND RAMPANT TORTURE

A woman in Pyongyang, North Korea, invited a few friends over for a "girls' night" in December 1992. They spent the evening having fun, enjoying each other's company, and singing songs. The hostess didn't know her neighbor was one of

Above: 15 Communist prisoners in large maximum security cell, United Nations POW camp number 1, Koje-Do, North Korea. US Army photograph, December 11, 1952, during the Korean war

North Korea's many informants, nor that he had been listening to the women with his ear pressed up against the wall.

Days later, the woman was arrested and taken to the People's Safety Agency jail, where she was beaten and sexually abused for three years. Each of her friends was sentenced to eight months of hard labor in a prison camp. The women were being punished for "singing the wrong song" that night. The offending song, "Don't Cry, Hongdo," was a South Korean pop tune. The government said that singing it showed disloyalty to the Kim Jong-il regime, a crime that carries the most severe penalties in North Korea. Informants, such as the woman's neighbor, assist in enforcing the law by tattling on their neighbors, a common practice in Stalin's Soviet Union that was adopted by North Korea in the 1940s.

The woman arrested for singing was former North Korean singer Ji Hae Nam. Her three-year sentence might have been longer, but she was granted clemency and pardoned to celebrate the 50th anniversary of Korea's liberation from Japan. Unfortunately, however, her nightmare recommenced. Nam was unable to get work when she returned to Pyongyang, so she escaped to China in 1998. There,

SOVIET SYSTEM

In Russia under Stalin, millions were imprisoned in the gulags. The system was created in 1919, and by 1936 five million people were interned. The total number of people who were sent to the gulag is not known, though estimates range from 15 to 30 million.

a human sex trafficker kidnapped and sold her to a man who locked her in his home and forced her to be his sex slave for seven months. Nam tried to flee by boat, but her vessel capsized, and Chinese officials spotted her struggling in the water. China repatriated Nam to North Korea, where she suffered for five weeks in a hell of physical and sexual abuse at a detention center before escaping to China again. This time, fortunately, she communicated with a pastor who helped her flee to Vietnam. Nam was finally able to seek asylum in the South Korean embassy in Hanoi. She currently resides in South Korea.

Nam's story is similar in many ways to those of the roughly 80,000 to 120,000 men, women, and children in the North Korean gulags today. Political prisoners, as well as ordinary criminals, are abducted in black vans throughout the country and tossed into hard-labor camps. They often receive no trial, and sometimes their sentence remains is unspecified. Victims of North Korea's arbitrary and inhumane penal system don't know if they will ever get out. Their day-to-day life becomes a ceaseless struggle.

PRISONS AND LABOR

Prisoners in the gulags of North Korea wake up well before dawn to perform factory jobs under the most appalling conditions. Lacking proper nourishment, they may eat substitutes such as grass, maggots, rats, snakes, and tree bark. Prisoners work all day, with breaks implemented only for the purpose of witnessing an execution, and they are frequently beaten and tortured by the guards. At night the prisoners are forced to confess the "sins" they committed that day, and if they have nothing to confess, they are punished for lying. If they do confess, however, they are forced to work harder, longer hours the next day to atone for their transgressions. Up to 80 prisoners sleep in 16 by 20 foot rooms, sometimes sitting up or standing all night. There is no plumbing and no bathing; lice, tuberculosis, malaria, and hepatitis are prevalent. Women are raped, and if they become pregnant they are beaten to induce stillbirths. If a repatriated female prisoner is pregnant when she arrives at the camp, the guards might allow her to have the baby only to torture and kill it in front of her.

The gulags of North Korea, collectively referred to as *kwalliso* in Korean, were built by the Soviet Union during its brief occupation of North Korea after World War II. The camps were made to punish, work, and reeducate enemies of the state, a penal system modeled after the one Stalin implemented in the Soviet Union. Following the Soviet model, the kwalliso were reserved for political dissenters and potential rivals to Kim Il-sung's leadership. In the camps, prisoners would learn how to toil in collective, ceaseless manual labor. Il-sung hoped they would be so utterly drained from torture, nonstop labor, degradation, and sleeplessness that their minds could be molded into the "juche man," an obedient child-of-the-state who would follow his governance unfailingly. Torture, beatings, rape, starvation, illness, and bitterly freezing weather added an additional dehumanizing element to the camps. Not much has changed in these camps in 21st century, except that they are getting bigger and more populated under the reign of Kim Jong-un.

Listening to a foreign radio station, sitting on a photo of Kim Jong-un, and making a negative comment about the government are all crimes in North Korea, punishable by a potential lifetime term in a gulag-style labor camp. Other political crimes condemned by the government include idleness in upholding communist principles.

In the 1990s, the 14 labor camps in North Korea grew to accommodate a population swelled by an increase in theft, escape attempts to China, and outspoken anti-government sentiment in response to famine and flood. Consequently, many camps were consolidated. Satellite images of North Korea now show four to six camps, each the size of a city, and all under the authority of the North Korea National Security Agency. The largest camp, Yoduk, is in South Hamgyong Province, 70 miles northeast of Pyongyang. Anti-aircraft guns are in place to repel external attacks, a thousand guards with fully automatic assault weapons patrol the perimeter, and the entire camp is enclosed in a minefield. As of 2012, an estimated 50,000 prisoners were held at Yoduk, but getting an accurate, up-to-date prisoner count of any kwalliso camp is not easy. The most accurate estimates come from satellite photos of the camps' size.

Guilt by association is one of the most paralyzing political policies in North Korea.

The National Security Agency divides Yoduk into "total control zones" for those serving life sentences and "reeducation" zones for those serving "revolutionary sentences." Prisoners in total control zones make it out alive only if they become so ill and frail that the agency allows them to wander off to die rather than having to dispose of their bodies. Pukchang, the oldest camp in North Korea, also has a revolutionary section for non-life sentences, but camps like Kaechon are just total control zones, where inmates never leave. Sunghon is reserved for the "incorrigibles," and defectors say it is the most feared of the camps. Former Sunghon prisoners have never publicly identified themselves, and so we can only speculate about what specifically occurs there. Some survivors of Kaechon have identified themselves, and most of them are the children and grandchildren of political dissidents. Guilt by association is one of the most paralyzing political policies in North Korea and has arguably been the greatest deterrent to an uprising. A North Korean defector calling himself Mr. Seo says, "If you have one life to live, you would gladly give it to overthrow this government, but you are not the only one getting punished. Your family will go through hell."

Psychological manipulation in North Korea is perpetuated by the songbun social hierarchal system, which normalizes the dehumanizing treatment of the lowest "hostile" class. Anyone in a prison camp is immediately regarded as a member of this class. Kwalliso guards, who are much more privileged because they work for the government, are conditioned to view inmates as subhuman. These guards are given college scholarships as incentives to murder, and so they have the capacity to shoot prisoners for sport. Since the economy depends so heavily on output from the kwalliso, guards purposefully push prisoners beyond exhaustion to fill quotas. They deprive prisoners of food for failure to produce goods at the rate expected, despite the fact that starvation increases fatigue and makes work more difficult.

The upper levels of the regime depend on these prisoners to produce boots, sweaters, jackets, and plastic flowers to trade with China. The Chinese government does not discourage this trade and ignores the human rights violations, in favor of the financial benefits of free labor from the kwalliso.

Human rights groups estimate that the vast majority of prisoners in the kwalliso labor camps are North Koreans. However, North Korea has a history of abducting foreigners from their home countries and forcing them to help the regime in some way. Most of these abducted foreigners were well-educated South Koreans and Japanese nationals who were made to contribute to North Korean intelligence agencies before they were imprisoned or, at best, allowed to blend into North Korean life. Abduction victims have been choked unconscious, silenced with oral anesthetics, thrown in sacks, and shipped alive to North Korea. According to the government of Japan, 17 Japanese nationals have been abducted since 1977. A 2014 UN Security Council investigation looked into these offshore Japanese abductions and found that they "occurred in the countryside, near the coast." The Council said, "Agents approach(ed) Japan by sea, and landed onshore. Women walking alone were often targeted for the ease at which they could be overcome." South Koreans are even easier targets for North Korean abduction missions, as there is no water barrier to cross. The South Korean government estimates the North has abducted over 3,800 nationals on their side of the 38th parallel since 1953. Escapes and negotiations with the North have brought only 480 South Koreans home. Since 2007, returning abductees have received financial assistance under the Law for the Victims of Abduction to the North in the Postwar Years. The North lies about where thousands of other abductees are and how they are being treated, making negotiations very challenging.

SEEKING INTERNATIONAL ACTION

To draw international attention to the human rights situation in North Korea, some groups have demanded accountability from

South Koreans hold their North Korean relatives' hands on a bus after the Separated Family Reunion Meeting at Diamond Mountain in North Korea, Tuesday, February 25, 2014.

North Korea. In 2014 the UN Human Rights Council adopted a resolution to address these issues, and in late 2014 the United Nations General Assembly made a motion to condemn North Korea for its crimes against humanity. This was a significant step toward bringing North Korean government officials to justice at the International Criminal Court. The Assembly presented findings from a special committee on the kwalliso, concluding that the camps are "without parallel in the contemporary world." The NGO Human Rights Watch is on board with the initiative to bring the Kim regime to justice and is prepared to lobby for the motion.

Jihyun Park, a former prisoner in North Korea, now works to bring awareness to human rights abuses in the country.

The Korean Central News Agency, North Korea's only news network, later delivered a statement from the Foreign Ministry that framed the movement to condemn their "nonexistent" labor camps as "aggression toward North Korea" from the United States. The movement was a threat to their juche ideals of isolationism, they said, and it would justify the perpetuation of North Korea's nuclear tests.

Amnesty International is assisting in putting a name and face to the suffering in North Korean labor camps. In 2015, when *The Interview* was released for home viewing, Amnesty International released *The Other Interview: Escape from North Korea*, a 15-minute documentary on the life of one North Korean refugee, Jihyun Park. She left North Korea during the 1990s famine and was sold into a slave marriage in China. After six years, authorities discovered her and repatriated her to North Korea, where she was sent to a labor camp. When she contracted tetanus in her leg, she was released to die in the streets. Park fled North Korea for a second time, and she trekked to Mongolia where she was able to seek asylum at the United Nations High Commission for Refugees office in Beijing. Today she lives with her children and husband in the United Kingdom. In *The Other Interview*, Park said of the camp and North Korea: "We were worked harder than animals. . . . Really, it was unspeakably bad. You could say the whole of North Korea is one big prison. The people were all hungry. There weren't even rats, snakes, or wild plants left for them to eat."

By sharing her experience, Park is giving a voice to the hundreds of thousands of prisoners who cannot speak for themselves. She also publicly supports the work of groups that are summoning world attention to the ongoing crimes of the North Korean state.

Defectors' testimony is one of the principle means of obtaining information about the conditions in the prison camps. There have been cases, however, where their accounts have proven inaccurate. Shin Dong-hyuk, whose story of escape from North Korea became the bestselling book Escape from Camp 14, stated that he had altered certain aspects of the story, including where he had been held and the timeline of certain events during his imprisonment. However, the abuses Shin suffered, such as seeing his mother and brother murdered by guards, were authentic. The maintenance of accuracy is key in exposing the brutal conditions of life in the gulags, as is understanding the excessive brutality of the Kim regime.

THIS IS THE END

전쟁은 시작될것이다

WHOSE FREE SPEECH?

CAN KIM JONG-UN EXERT CONTROL
BEYOND HIS BORDERS?

North Korea has attempted to assert creative control beyond its borders, most famously in the case of *The Interview* (2014), a satire about two journalists conscripted by the American government to assassinate Kim Jong-un. On June 25, 2014, the state-run Korean Central News Agency announced that the North Korean government would launch a "stern and merciless" retaliation if the movie went to theaters. A month later, they appealed to US president Barack Obama to ban the film. President Obama dismissed the request: The North Korean reaction spoke more about Jong-un's regime than the film itself, he said.

Nevertheless, the New York City premiere of *The Interview* was cancelled, and theater chains across the country, fearing potential acts of terror, refused to show it. This set off a wave of outrage among filmmakers, who felt the cancellation threatened their own freedom of expression. Larry Flynt, founder of *Hustler* magazine, said he would fight the oppression by making a pornographic parody called *This Ain't the Interview XXX*. "I've spent a lifetime fighting for the First Amendment," he said. "No foreign dictator is going to take my right to free speech."

Before *The Interview* was scheduled to go into theaters, the internal online network at Sony was hacked by a group calling themselves the Guardians of Peace. The Guardians leaked private emails about future Sony films to the public and sent their own messages to *The Interview*'s filmmakers, threatening them and theatergoers with acts of terror. North Korea officially denies involvement with the Sony hack incident, but some North Korean defectors say the hack was obviously the handiwork of Unit 121, North Korea's cyber-warfare agency. On February 17, 2015, after modifying the death scene, Sony released the film on DVD and Blu-ray disc.

MASS GAMES

HUGE GYMNASTICS EVENTS PROMOTE THE KIM LEGEND, BUT PLAYERS FAR OUTNUMBER THE AUDIENCE

"Mass gymnastics foster particularly healthy and strong physiques, a high degree of organization, discipline, and collectivism in schoolchildren," Kim Jong-il said in a 1987 speech. The outcome is mass gymnastics events in North Korea at the 2.2-million-square-foot Rungrado May 1 (May Day) Stadium in Pyongyang, which can involve up to 100,000 dancer-gymnasts. The most famous of these events is the Arirang Festival, which tells the story of a couple forced apart by an evil landlord, a breakup roughly analogous to the Korean War. Symbols in the show, such as a giant sun, are iconographic of Kim Il-sung and Jong-il's birth and life.

Arirang events are highly politicized and very well choreographed. The strict choreography connects the individuals in lockstep, demonstrating their singular ideology. Since these events are so enormous, they can only really be appreciated from far away, and performers usually far outnumber spectators. This is acceptable to the Kims, who are sometimes the only ones in attendance.

Similar displays celebrate the two most important national holidays: The Day of Sun (Kim Il-sung's birthday) and The Day of the Shining Star (Kim Jong-il's birthday). Dance exhibitions, military parades, and patriotic chants are held in the streets of Pyongyang to delight and excite the current leader, Jong-un.

Left: A ray of light during the "Prosper Our Country" mass games in Pyongyang stadium. Below: A North Korean myth is recounted by a huge image created by thousands of children. It represents the two pistols reportedly used by Kim Il-sung when he founded the Anti-Japanese People's Guerrilla Army in 1932.

REPUBLIC OF REPRESSION

NORTH KOREANS LIVE CONTINUOUSLY WATCHED BY THE GOVERNMENT

Pyongyang is the pride of the Democratic People's Republic of Korea. Its urban planning provides for a wide thoroughfare, skyscrapers, and a plethora of artistic monuments devoted to the Great Leader Kim Il-sung and his successor, the Dear Leader Kim Jong-il. The city's populace seems to bustle along at a steady pace: college students walking the campus of Kim Il-sung University, young women shopping for the latest fashions, children skipping through the streets after school, and office workers smoking cigarettes outside government buildings. To any foreign visitor, Pyongyang might appear to be a modern city, but spending a little time there and looking more scrupulously with a keen eye soon reveals the city's peculiarities. For instance, cars rarely drive down Pyongyang's wide thoroughfares, and the streets are not just clean, they're sterile. The dimly lit shops are all in pristine, grand-opening order, and the 105-story pyramidal hotel marking the skyline is mostly vacant. Indeed, the hustle and bustle that foreign visitors see is staged for their benefit. Real civilian life in North Korea is nothing at all like the urban scenes so carefully orchestrated for tourists.

Left: The wide, empty streets of Kaesong, totally devoid of traffic

What little the outside world knows of North Korea comes from defectors, refugees, and tourists, and although foreigners are not welcome, the government occasionally allows their visits in hope of generating good press. To this end, they are sure to "clean up" any unpleasant sights before guests arrive, and tourists are watched closely throughout their stay. Agent Koh of North Korea's National Security Police accompanied Mike Kim, the founder of Crossing Borders Ministries in China, during his four-day visit to North Korea. When Kim tried to photograph the starving orphaned children approaching him for money, Koh instructed, "Only take pictures that make us look good so that when you return home you can tell everyone how beautiful our country is." Such an order undermines the government's expressed belief in its own greatness, and yet it is precisely this kind of hypocrisy that maintains the status quo in North Korea.

> *The government makes every effort to keep North Koreans from engaging with the outside world.*

Although scenes of normal life in Pyongyang appear staged for tourists, the real inhabitants are drawn from the "loyal" class of North Korea's three-tiered social hierarchy, and they are afforded the highest standard of living in the country. The system, called songbun, governs the kind of food, education, employment, and housing each person receives. Most North Koreans belong to the peasant or "wavering" class. Beneath them is the "hostile" class, composed of former landowners, business people, pro-Japanese colonial collaborators, criminals, and family members of defectors. People are locked into their class based on the actions of their ancestors. Kim Il-sung instituted a policy of punishing the relatives of those he deemed political dissidents. Kim Jong-il relaxed this rule to apply only in cases of major shows of disloyalty. At best, they will live lives of poverty and disease in the far north. While social class determines the kinds of luxuries or degree of deprivation that people face in their lifetime, North Korean civil laws are universally restrictive. The government makes every effort to keep North Koreans from engaging with the outside world, to effectively mitigate the development of revolutionary thoughts and ideas among the populace. One way this is accomplished is by observing the North Korean people in real time on closed-circuit television monitors. The Ministry of State Security uses carefully worded propaganda to present their supervision under the guise of a loving parent. Within the juche ideology, where Kim Jong-un is regarded as the nation's father, this rationale makes sense.

ISOLATION AND SECURITY

Being cut off from the outside world is a fact of life in North Korea. Since the end of World War II, and with it the Japanese occupation,

Foreign visitors are taken to Christian churches to see that North Korea allows religious diversity and fully exercises tolerance for all religions. However, because religious worship is illegal and considered grounds for treason in North Korea, no services are ever held in the churches. The churches themselves are strictly props utilized for the purpose of promoting the illusion of tolerance.

the North has insisted on isolation as a form of protection from the occupation and hegemony of outside nations. While the South reconciled sovereignty with globalization, the North deems these concepts mutually exclusive. International trade was out of the question for Kim Il-sung, who pursued a closed economy in the context of which North Korea would be completely self-reliant. In Il-sung's Korea, the populace worked for the common goal of strengthening the military. The collectivist agenda obviated the need for money, and everyone was supposed to be fed, clothed, and sheltered by the government. Loyalty to the regime became the most important currency in this society, and with people's survival needs depending on loyalty, the system has worked well for Il-sung and his successors.

One of the greatest dangers to the Kim cult of personality is interaction with the outside world. The North Korean propaganda machine insists that the rest of the world envies life in North Korea and that Kim Jong-un is protecting North Koreans from real deprivation and hardship. Lies about foreign hostility to North Korea are an important addendum to the apocryphal protection narrative, as they help the North Korean people make sense of the songun policy adopted in 1995. With North Korea's militarization efforts taking full precedence over feeding and clothing the populace, any North Korean person disagreeing with the military-first policy potentially faces a life of imprisonment.

With the expression of individuality discouraged from early childhood, the North Korean people likely do not know how to oppose the regime. "Brainwashing starts in the womb," a North Korean defector told BBC's John Sweeny in his documentary *North Korea Undercover*. "It becomes natural to bow to the Kims every morning." Preschool children in North Korea are taught to love Kim Jong-un

North Korean students who were selected as delegates to the Korean Children's Union pay their respects in front of bronze statues of late North Korean leaders Kim Il-sung and Kim Jong-il in Pyongyang, North Korea.

more than their parents. They are told that their love for him will ensure they have books, toys, and food for the rest of their lives. Such early childhood indoctrination is supposed to fuse survival with loyalty to the Kims.

The perpetual socioeconomic crises in North Korea, however, have forced many North Koreans into stealing, bribing, and black marketeering as a way of surviving. Higher-end salaries average about US $3 per month. In addition, government employees cannot be sure they will be paid at the end of the month, as arbitrary labor laws can capriciously and indefinitely withhold wages. Some people have made ends meet by illegally selling produce or seafood, but these aren't lucrative trades, and the ever-depreciating value of the North Korean won makes it more difficult to sell goods every year. At the same time, families still need to eat, and

South Korean protesters hold signs and shout slogans during a rally demanding that China stop repatriating North Korean asylum seekers.

some North Korean people ultimately turn to theft as a way of staying alive. Since the 1990s, stealing has been an essential survival tactic and has become a customary facet of North Korean society. "Everyone steals from each other over there . . . If you can't do something bad, you are naive and you won't survive," 16-year-old defector Kyung Hwa told Mike Kim of Crossing Borders Ministries after he helped her flee from North Korea.

Bribery has also been normalized and is considered one of the only ways to travel around the country. Travel permits are required to leave a person's town of birth, and permit applications are frequently "lost" or discarded. Officials, however, are eager to accept bribes instead of upholding the law. The economy also encourages black marketeering, which usually involves drug dealing, selling goods, or human trafficking between North Korea and China. While a person can be sentenced to life in prison for sitting on a picture of Kim Jong-un, black marketeering is commonly condoned. The government reasons that leniency for offenders is counterbalanced by the foreign currency their illegal activities bring into North Korea. Indeed, the cult of personality is actively cultivating depravity. Low-quality, affordable alcohol is the only available item on most store shelves, and crystal meth use is prevalent among men ages 17 and older. Drug and alcohol addiction is common in the rural areas of North Korea, where people are trapped in their hometowns without jobs, farms, education, or a sense of purpose.

THE STRUGGLE TO LEAVE

Despite the Kim regime's efforts, an unknown number of refugees escape North Korea every year. The 1951 United Nations Refugee Convention protects refugees from repatriation to oppressive regimes such as North Korea, and the countries that signed on to the convention are considered refugee "safe havens." China is a signatory of the convention, but a 1986 bilateral agreement between Beijing and Pyongyang has undercut China's duty to fulfill the conditions of the convention. When the pact was made, China was experiencing a massive influx of "distress migration" from North Korea as people fled from the impending famine. Fearing that the North Koreans might cause unemployment and

The Emergency The health care system is so bankrupt that North Korean doctors barter their medical services for food, alcohol, and cigarettes.

MOVING STORY

Crossing (2008), directed by Kim Tae-kyun, is a film about a North Korean man crossing the border into China in search of medicine for his ailing wife, who dies before he is able to successfully reach safety. It won film awards in South Korea, where it was produced, and it was submitted as a foreign language entry to the Academy Awards. It was not among the final nominees.

instability, China refused to recognize them as refugees. Beijing therefore signed the 1986 agreement with Pyongyang so China could legally send the refugees back to North Korea. Having committed one of the worst crimes, that of leaving the country, most repatriated North Koreans are forced to spend the rest of their lives in labor camps with no judicial recourse.

Life outside the labor camps is arduous for most. Even if the poorest North Koreans could afford a visit to the doctor, the health care system is so dilapidated that hospitals reuse hypodermic needles, operate on people without anesthesia, and can provide only black-market medicine. Preventable diseases such as malaria, typhoid fever, and tuberculosis run rampant in the most poverty-stricken areas of the northern countryside. Instead of addressing these issues, the government insists on building armaments and pursuing the advancement of nuclear weapons.

The Kim family and the Korean Workers' Party respond to every issue with a different version of the same rhetoric. From their point of view, people bring suffering on themselves by being disloyal to Kim Jong-un and must consequently pay with their lives, their children's lives, and their grandchildren's lives. No one is safe to speak, move, or think in North Korea without putting his or her limited freedom in jeopardy, and even humanitarian aid organizations can be corrupt.

To those living outside North Korea, the situation can seem abstract. *Oppression* is less harsh without the sound of individual cries, and the Kims have gagged an entire nation. *Starvation* can be difficult to understand for people who have never been hungry, and the Kims have made it invisible. Perhaps their isolation is a blessing to North Koreans, since just across the Demilitarized Zone, so close and yet so far away, people with the same cultural legacy are thriving. Yet the electronics and digital revolution that has brought so much prosperity to the South may eventually be the undoing of the Kim Dynasty. When information is the greatest threat to a regime, a single tablet or cell phone may end up being more powerful than Kim Jung-un's weapons of mass destruction and repression.

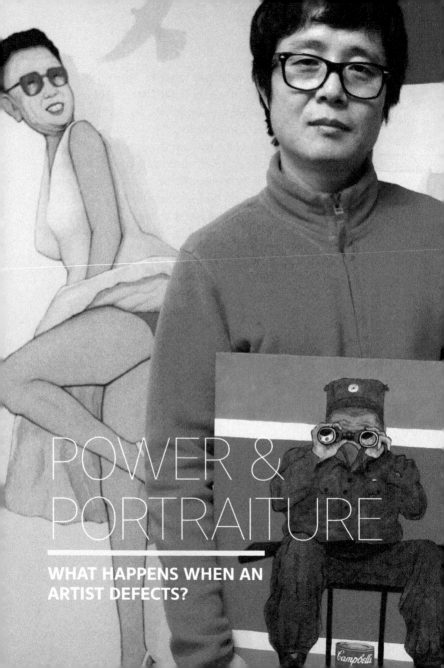

POWER & PORTRAITURE

**WHAT HAPPENS WHEN AN
ARTIST DEFECTS?**

When he lived in Pyongyang, artist Song Byeok painted portraits of Kim Il-sung, which is essentially the only thing about his life that hasn't changed since he fled North Korea in 2001. Once a revered Party member and propaganda artist, Song was imprisoned after crossing the border into China in search of food during the 1990s, nearly starved to death, and subsequently defected. Now a resident of South Korea and fervently anti-Kim, Song subverts the dynasty he once praised, using exactly the same medium. His most famous work, "Take Off Your Clothes," shows Kim Jong-il's head on the body of Marilyn Monroe. He frequently uses white birds as symbols of freedom, usually depicted against something official-looking, such as a soldier or a mass dance demonstration.

A PARTING THOUGHT

"Comrades, the great 100-year history of the Kim Il-sung nation is a history that proves the iron truth that dignity and great prosperity of a country and nation exist only when an excellent leader is served."

—KIM JONG-UN

SOURCES

Amnesty International. "The Other Interview: Escape from North Korea."
    February 6, 2015. Accessed April 25, 2015. www.amnestyusa.org/news
    /news-item/the-other-interview-escape-from-north-korea
————. "The Other Interview: Escape from North Korea." YouTube
    www.youtube.com/watch?v=DMn2_2TxiSw

Anderson, Ericka. "North Korea to Olympians: No Medals Means
    Labor Camp." DailySignal. August 8, 2012. Accessed April 12, 2015.
    dailysignal.com/2012/08/08/north-korea-to-olympians-no-medals
    -means-labor-camp/

Armstrong, Charles. *The North Korean Revolution, 1945–50.* Ithaca, NY:
    Cornell University Press, 2013.

Asia for Educators. "Korea as a Colony of Japan (1910–1945)."
    Accessed June 21, 1015. afe.easia.columbia.edu/main_pop/kpct
    /kp_koreaimperialism.htm

Barron, Brian. "West Snubs North Korea Movies." BBC News.
    September 5, 2001. Accessed April 22, 2015. news.bbc.co.uk/2/hi
    /entertainment/1526628.stm

Bix, Herbert P. *Hirohito and the Making of Modern Japan.* New York, NY:
    Harper Collins, 2009.

Boot, William. "Exclusive: Sony E-mails Say State Department Blessed
    Kim Jong-Un Assassination in 'The Interview.'" The Daily Beast.
    December 19, 2011. Accessed April 23, 2014. www.thedailybeast.com
    /articles/2014/12/17/exclusive-sony-emails-allege-u-s-govt-official
    -ok-d-controversial-ending-to-the-interview.html

Buzo, Adrian. *The Making of Modern Korea.* Routledge: New York, NY, 2002.

Cain, Geoffrey. "White Supremacists and Spanish Spokesmen: Meet Kim
    Jong Un's BFFs." NBC News. December 2, 2014. Accessed April 24, 2015.
    www.nbcnews.com/news/world/white-supremacists-spanish
    -spokesman-meet-kim-jong-uns-bffs-n259566

Caprio, Mark. *Japanese Assimilation Policies in Colonial Korea, 1910–1945.* Seattle,
    WA: University of Washington Press, 2014.

Carter, Jimmy. Frontline, PBS. Accessed August 11, 2015 http://www.pbs.org
    /wgbh/pages/frontline/shows/kim/interviews/carter.html

Casey, Michael. "Korean DMZ Proves Unlikely Wildlife Haven." *Los Angeles
    Times.* June 4, 2006. articles.latimes.com/2006/jun/04/news/adfg-dmz21

Cha, Victor. *The Impossible State: North Korea, Past and Future.* New York, NY:
    Harper Collins, 2012.

CNN. "Kim Il-Sung's Quest to Live to 100." YouTube. www.youtube.com
    /watch?v=rB9p9S0RGXQ

Country Listing. "North Korea: The Judiciary." Accessed June 21, 2015.
www.country-data.com/cgi-bin/query/r-9648.html

Dao, James. "Aftereffects: Asian Arena; North Korea Is Said to Export Drugs to Get Foreign Currency," *The New York Times*. May 21, 2003.

Dejohn, Irving. "Kim Jong Un Orders All Relatives of Executed Uncle to be Killed: Report." *Daily News*. January 27, 2014. Accessed April 25, 2015. www.nydailynews.com/news/world/kim-jong-executes-uncle -relatives-report-article-1.1592385

Demick, Barbara. *Nothing to Envy: Ordinary Lives in North Korea*. New York, NY: Speigel & Grau, 2009.

European Union. "EU Relations with the Democratic People's Republic of Korea." Accessed April 25, 2015. eeas.europa.eu/korea_north/index_en.htm

European Union Delegation to the United Nations. "Outcomes of the 28th Human Rights Council." March 27, 2015. Accessed April 25, 2015. eu-un.europa.eu/articles/en/article_16265_en.htm

Fehrenbach, T. R. *This Kind of War: The Classic Military History of the Korean War*. New York, NY: Open Road, 2014.

Fisher, Max. "North Korea's Gulags: A Horror 'Without Any Parallel in the Contemporary World.'" Vox. February 5, 2015. Accessed April 25, 2015. www.vox.com/2014/10/27/7073029/north-korea-gulags-prison -camps-explainer

Fenton, Siobhan. "Kim Jong-un Claims to Have Cured Aids, Ebola and Cancer with Single Miracle Drug," *The Independent*. Accessed June 20, 2015. www.independent.co.uk/news/world/asia/kim-jongun-claims-to-have -cured-aids-ebola-and-cancer-with-single-miracle-drug-10332386.html

Fifield, Anna. "North Korea, Angry over Human Rights Pressures, Threatens Another Nuclear Test." *The Washington Post*. November 20, 2014. Accessed April 25, 2015. www.washingtonpost.com/world/angry-over -human-rights-pressures-north-korea-threatens-another-nuclear -test/2014/11/20/1bee71f8-8ee7-47ac-a15f-873d36a6c322_story.html

Fifield, Anna. "North Korea Begins Brainwashing Children in Cult of the Kims as Early as Kindergarten." *The Washington Post*. January 16. Accessed June 21, 2015. www.washingtonpost.com/world/asia_pacific/for-north -koreas-kims-its-never-too-soon-to-start-brainwashing/2015/01/15 /a23871c6-9a67-11e4-86a3-1b56f64925f6_story.html

Frayer, Lauren. "The Spanish Aristocrat Who Works for North Korea." Parallels. July 20, 2013. Accessed April 24, 2015. www.npr.org/blogs /parallels/2013/07/20/195590639/the-spanish-aristocrat-who-works -for-north-korea

Freemuse. "Three Years in Prison for Simply Singing a Wrong Song." 2009. Accessed April 25, 2015. freemuse.org/archives/1254

French, Paul. *North Korea: The Paranoid Peninsula: A Modern History*. Second Edition. London, UK: Zed Books, 2007.

Gibbs, Samuel. "Did North Korea's Notorious Unit 121 Cyber Army Hack Sony Pictures?" *The Guardian*. December 2, 2014. Accessed April 12, 2015. www.theguardian.com/technology/2014/dec/02/north-korea-hack -sony-pictures-brad-pitt-fury

Global Security. "Operation Paul Bunyan: Tree / Hatchet Incident 18 August 1976." Accessed June 21, 2015. www.globalsecurity.org/military/ops /paul_bunyan.htm

Gluckman, Ron. "Cinema Stupido." Gluckman. 1992. Accessed April 22, 2015. www.gluckman.com/NKfilm.html

Greenberg, Andy. "The Plot to Free North Korea with Smuggled Episodes of 'Friends.'" Wired. March 1, 2015. www.wired.com/2015/03/north-korea/

"Gulag." Encyclopedia Britannica, ed. Accessed August 5, 2015. www.britannica.com/place/Gulag

Hawk, David. "The Hidden Gulag, Second Edition." The Committee for Human Rights in North Korea. www.hrnk.org/uploads/pdfs /HRNK_HiddenGulag2_Web_5-18.pdf Accessed August 3, 2015.

Herman, Steve. "North Korea: Ten Years Later." Asian Research. Accessed April 12, 2015. www.asianresearch.org/articles/2209.html

Human Rights Watch. *Human Rights in North Korea*. Accessed April 25, 2015. www.hrw.org/nkorea

———— .World Report 2015. www.hrw.org/world-report/2015/country-chapters /north-korea?page=1

Judkis, Maura. "North Korean artist Song Byeok: from propaganda painter to political refugee." The Washington Post. Accessed August 3, 2015. www.washingtonpost.com/lifestyle/style/north-korean-artist -song-byeok-from-propaganda-painter-to-political-refugee /2012/04/13/gIQA4IYkFT_story.html

Kilday, Gregg. "Sony Hack: Carmike Cinema Drops 'The Interview.'" *The Hollywood Reporter*. December 17, 2015. Accessed April 23, 2015. www.hollywoodreporter.com/news/sony-hack-carmike-cinemas -drops-758444

Kaiman, Jonathan. "Story about Kim Jong-un's Uncle Being Fed to Dogs Orig-inated with Satirist." *The Guardian*. January 6, 2014. Accessed July 7, 2015. www.theguardian.com/world/2014/jan/06/story-kim-jong-un-uncle -fed-dogs-made-up

Kim, Eugene. "We Spoke to a North Korean Defector Who Trained with Its Hackers—What He Said Is Pretty Scary." *Business Insider*. December 24, 2014. Accessed April 23, 2014. www.businessinsider.com/north-korean -defector-jang-se-yul-trained-with-hackers-2014-12

Kim, Il-sung. *BrainyQuote*. Accessed June 21, 2015. www.brainyquote.com /quotes/quotes/k/kimilsung220067.html

Kim, Il-sung. "For a free and peaceful new world." Marxist Internet Archives. Accessed August 3, 2015. www.marxists.org/archive /kim-il-sung/1991/04/29.htm

Kim, Jong-il. *Encyclopedia Britannica*. Accessed Jun 21, 2015. www.britannica.com /biography/Kim-Jong-Il

Kim, Jong-un. Speech on April 15, 2012, as translated by Martyn Williams. North Korea Tech. Accessed August 3, 2015. www.northkoreatech.org /2012/04/18/english-transcript-of-kim-jong-uns-speech/

Kim, Mike. *Escaping North Korea: Defiance and Hope in the World's Most Repressive Country*. Lanham, MD: Rowman & Littlefield, 2008.

Kim, Suk-Young. *DMZ Crossing: Performing Emotional Citizenship Along the Korean Border*. New York, NY: Columbia University Press, 2014.

Kit, Borys. "Dennis Rodman Opens Up About 'The Interview,' Invites Seth Rogen to North Korea." *The Hollywood Reporter*. January 24, 2015. Accessed April 24, 2015. www.hollywoodreporter.com/news/dennis -rodman-opens-up-interview-766651

Korea4Expats. "Symbolism of Korean Flag." Accessed June 21, 2015. http://www.korea4expats.com/article-korean-flag-symbolism.html

Lankov, Andrei. *From Stalin to Kim Il Sung: The Formation of North Korea*. New Brunswick, NJ: Rutgers University Press, 2002.

——— ."The Surprising News from North Korea's Prisons." Bloomberg View. Accessed August 3, 2015. www.bloombergview.com/articles/2014-10-13 /life-beyond-north-korea-s-gulag

Lee, Bong. *The Unfinished War: Korea*. New York, NY: Agora Publishing, 2003.

MacLeod, Calum. "Korean Defectors Recall 'Day of the Sun'." *USA Today*. April 26, 2013. Accessed April 18, 2014. www.usatoday.com/story/news /world/2013/04/15/north-korea-defectors/2085161/

Martin, Bradley K. *Under the Loving Care of the Fatherly Leader: North Korea and the Kim Dynasty*. New York, NY: Thomas Dunne Books, 2004.

Matheison, Craig. "Aim High in Creation!: Anna Broinowski Interview." SBS. February 24, 2015. Accessed April 22, 2015. www.sbs.com.au/movies /article/2014/03/31/aim-high-creation-anna-broinowski-interview

McKenna, Bill. "North Korean propaganda artist Song Byeok turns satirist." BBC.com. Accessed August 3, 2015. www.bbc.com/news /magazine-20500030

Meyer, Milton S. *Japan: A Concise History*. Lanham, MD: Rowman & Littlefield, 2013.

Min, Choi Song. "North Korea Introduces Mandatory Military Service for Women." *The Guardian*. July 31, 2015. Accessed April 21, 2015. www.theguardian.com/world/2015/jan/31/north-korea-mandatory -military-service-women

National Association for the Rescue of Japanese Kidnapped by North Korea. "North Korean Abduction Victims Worldwide." Accessed April 25, 2015. www.sukuukai.jp/narkn/

National Geographic. "Inside North Korea." Documentary. Accessed April 21, 2015. https://www.youtube.com/watch?v=mxLBywKrTf4

Neville, Ted. "Happy Birthday? North Korea Celebrates Kim Jong Il's Legacy." CNN. February 15, 2015. Accessed April 24, 2015. www.cnn.com /2015/02/15/travel/gallery/kim-jong-il-birthday-travel/

Nuclear Threat Initiative, "North Korea." Accessed August 25, 2015. www.nti.org/country-profiles/north-korea/

O'Neill, Tom. "Korea's DMZ: Dangerous Divide." *National Geographic*. July 2003. Accessed June 21, 2015. ngm.nationalgeographic.com/print/features /world/asia/north-korea/dmz-text

Park, Kyung-Ae, and Snyder, Scott. *North Korea in Transition: Politics, Economy, and Society*. Lanham, MD: Rowman & Littlefield, 2013.

Portal, Jane. *Art Under Control in North Korea*. London, UK: Reaktion Books, 2005.

Postmedia Network. "Kim Jong-Un Claims to Have Scaled 9,000-ft Mountain." *Toronto Sun*. April 19, 2015. Accessed April 21, 2015. www.torontosun.com /2015/04/19/kim-jong-un-claims-to-have-scaled-9000-ft-mountain

Provost, Claire, and Simon Rogers. "Corruption Index 2011 from Transparency International: Find Out How Countries Compare." *The Guardian*. December 1, 2011. Accessed April 24, 2015. www.theguardian.com/news /datablog/2011/dec/01/corruption-index-2011-transparency-international

Rauhala, Emily. "Party in Pyongyang." *Time*. April 15, 2013. Accessed June 15, 2015. world.time.com/2013/04/15/party-in-pyongyang-amid-tension -north-korea-celebrates-kim-il-sungs-birthday/

Reynolds, Emma. "How Kim Jong-Il Kidnapped Movie Royalty and Forced Them to Make His Films." February 6, 2015. Accessed April 22, 2015. www.news.com.au/entertainment/books-magazines/how-kim-jong

-il-kidnapped-movie-royalty-and-forced-them-to-make-his-films
/story-fna50uae-1227210112984

RT. "Entire Family of Kim Jong-Un's Uncle Executed in N. Korea—Reports."
January 28, 2014. Accessed April 24, 2015. rt.com/news/korean-leader
-family-slayed-213/

Rundle, Michael. "Kim Jong-il: 18 Strange 'Facts' About the North Korean
Leader." *Huffington Post*. December 19, 2011. Accessed April 21, 2015.
www.huffingtonpost.co.uk/2011/12/19/kim-jong-il-18-strange-facts
_n_1157276.html

Sanger, David E. "Kenneth Bae and Matthew Todd Miller, Release by North
Korea, Are Back on US Soil." *The New York Times*. November 8, 2014.
Accessed April 24, 2015. www.nytimes.com/2014/11/09/world/kenneth
-bae-matthew-todd-miller-released-by-north-korea.html?_r=0

Savage, Mark. "Kim Jong-il: The Cinephile Despot." *BBC News*. December 19, 2011.
Accessed April 22, 2015. www.bbc.com/news/entertainment-arts-16245174

Schonner, Johannes. *North Korean Cinema: A History*. Jefferson, NC:
McFarland, 2012.

Sedghi, Ami, and Simon Rogers. "South v North Korea: How Do the Two Countries Compare? Visualized." *The Guardian*. April 8, 2013. www.theguardian
.com/world/datablog/2013/apr/08/south-korea-v-north-korea-compared

Sharpe, M.E. *North Korea Handbook*. Seoul, South Korea: Yonhap News
Agency, 2002.

Schoichet, Catherine. "North Korean prison camp survivor admits
inaccuracies, author says." CNN. Accessed August 3, 2015. www.cnn.com
/2015/01/18/asia/north-korea-defector-changes-story/

Smith, Lydia. "Kim Il-Sung Death Anniversary: How the North Korea Founder
Created a Cult of Personality." *International Business Times*. July 8, 2014.
Accessed April 15, 2015. www.ibtimes.co.uk/kim-il-sung-death-anniversary
-how-north-korea-founder-became-cult-personality-1455758

Stewart, Richard, ed. *American Military History Volume II: The United States
Army in a Global Era, 1917–2003*. The US Army Center of Military History.
Washington, DC, 2005.

Sthankiya, Nayan. "Korean 'Tigerman' Prowls the DMZ." OhMyNews!
December 12, 2004. Accessed April 21, 2015. english.ohmynews.com
/articleview/article_view.asp?menu=c10400&no=199457&rel_no=1

Stoddard, Katy. "North Korea: 10 Facts About One of the World's Most
Secretive States." *The Guardian*. December 19, 2011. www.theguardian.com
/news/datablog/2011/dec/19/north-korea-facts-secretive-state

Stone, Daniel. "New Space Station Photos Show North Korea at Night, Cloaked in Darkness." *National Geographic*. February 27, 2014. Accessed April 21, 2015. news.nationalgeographic.com/news /2014/02/140226-north-korea-satellite-photos-darkness-energy/

Sukuukai. "The Abduction of Japanese Nationals by North Korea." Accessed April 25, 2015. www.sukuukai.jp/English/Abductions.html

Szalontai, Balazs. *Kim Il Sung in the Krushchev Era: Soviet-DPRK Relations and the Roots of North Korean Despotism*. Redwood City, CA: Stanford University Press, 2005.

Szoldra, Paul. "South Korean 'Tunnel Hunters' Fear Surprise Attack by North Korea." *Business Insider*. March 11, 2013. Accessed Jun 21, 2015. www.businessinsider.com/war-north-and-south -korea-underground-2013-3

Taylor, Adam. "Torture, Kidnappings, and Gulags: North Korea's Alleged Crimes Against Humanity." *The Washington Post*. November 20, 2014. Accessed April 25, 2015. www.washingtonpost.com/blogs/worldviews /wp/2014/11/20/torture-kidnapping-and-gulags-north-koreas-alleged -crimes-against-humanity/

The Telegraph. "50 Fascinating Facts: Kim Jong-Il and North Korea." December 19, 2011. Accessed April 21, 2015. www.telegraph.co.uk/news/worldnews/asia /northkorea/8965694/50-fascinating-facts-Kim-Jong-il-and-North-Korea.html

The Telegraph. "North Korea Celebrates Birth/Anniversary of Founder Kim Il-Sung." April 16, 2015. Accessed June 21, 2015. www.telegraph.co.uk /news/worldnews/asia/northkorea/11537200/North-Korea-celebrates -birth-anniversary-of-founder-Kim-Il-sung.html

US Department of State, Office of the Historian. "Milestones: 1945–1952" Accessed July 7, 2015. https://history.state.gov/milestones/1945-1952 /korean-war-2

USA Today. "20 Facts About North Korea." April 13, 2013. Accessed April 24, 2015. www.usatoday.com/story/news/world/2013/04/13/north-korea -factoids/2078831/

Vargas, Marc. "Alejandro Cao de Benos: North Korea's Friend from the West." *International Business Times*. February 18, 2014. Accessed April 24, 2015. www.ibtimes.co.uk/alejandro-cao-de-benos-wests-friend-north -korea-1436968

INDEX

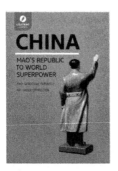

CPSIA information can be obtained at www.ICGtesting.com
Printed in the USA
BVOW11s0443080915

416165BV00003B/3/P